THE LIMITS OF DISSENT

THE LIMITS OF DISSENT

THE CONSTITUTIONAL STATUS OF ARMED CIVILIAN MILITIAS

Thomas Halpern
Brian Levin

with a foreword by
Charles E. Schumer

ALETHEIA PRESS
AMHERST, MASSACHUSETTS

Aletheia Press
Amherst, Massachusetts 01004

Cover photograph by Randy Bennett, Public Information Office, City of Oklahoma City, Oklahoma.

The views expressed by Brian Levin in this book do not necessarily reflect those of the Southern Poverty Law Center.

Manufactured in the United States of America.

Library of Congress Cataloging-in-Publication Data

Halpern, Thomas.
The limits of dissent : the constitutional status of armed civilian militias / Thomas Halpern, Brian Levin.
   p.   cm. — (The Law and Violence series : no. 3)
Includes bibliographical references
ISBN 1-880831-17-1 (pbk. : alk. paper)
   1. United States—Constitutional law—Amendments—2nd.
2. Military law—United States. 3. United States—Militia.
4. Freedom of speech—United States. 5. Firearms—Law and States.
6. Government, Resistance to—United States. 7. Militia movements—United States. 8. Political violence—United States. I. Levin, Brian.
II. Title. III. Series.
KF4558 2nd.H35 1996
343.73'015—dc20
[347.30315]

                                                              96-1095
                                                                 CIP

CONTENTS

CONTRIBUTORS

THOMAS HALPERN is Acting Director of Fact Finding for the Anti-Defamation League in New York, and an expert on extremist groups. He coordinates ADL's efforts to monitor and counteract anti-Semitism, racism, and extremism of both the far right and the far left, including the activities of armed militias, the Ku Klux Klan, neo-Nazi Skinheads, and Louis Farrakhan's Nation of Islam. Halpern has coauthored several ADL publications, and has spoken on ADL's role in combating extremism before law enforcement conferences around the country. He is an honors graduate of Harvard University.

BRIAN LEVIN is Associate Director for Legal Affairs at the Southern Poverty Law Center's Klanwatch Project in Montgomery, Alabama. He began his career as a New York City police officer in the Harlem-Washington Heights area of Manhattan. After graduating with multiple honors from the University of Pennsylvania, Levin received his law degree from Stanford University, where he was given the Block Civil Liberties Award for his research on hate crimes. Levin has testified as an expert before Congress on hate crime and domestic terrorism. He also has authored numerous widely cited scholarly articles.

CHARLES E. SCHUMER represents the Ninth Congressional District in Brooklyn and Queens in the U.S. House of Representatives.

HOWARD FRIEL is Publisher and Editor of Aletheia Press.

ACKNOWLEDGMENTS

My deepest gratitude to my wife, Lucy, for her constant love and support; and to my parents, for their love and wisdom. I also extend my sincere thanks and appreciation to my friends and colleagues at the Anti-Defamation League, including staff members and lay leaders both in New York and associated with our regional offices around the country. Among these I especially wish to thank Abraham H. Foxman, David H. Strassler, Robert Sugarman, Mira Jacobson, Jeffrey P. Sinensky, Irwin Suall, David Rosenberg, Mira L. Boland, Alan M. Schwartz, Gail L. Gans, Steven M. Freeman, and Yvonne Mentore.

—Thomas Halpern

I want to thank my parents for their support and moral guidance. I also wish to thank M.C. Sungaila for her support, encouragement, and editorial assistance. Her brilliant insights were instrumental to this effort. I am also indebted to Tom Diaz for his wise counsel, and Bettina Moss for her assistance. Thanks also to my many friends and colleagues at the Southern Poverty Law Center, especially Morris Dees, Richard Cohen, Angie Lowry, Joe Roy, Mike Reynolds, Laurie Wood, and the rest of the Klanwatch/Militia Task Force staff.

—Brian Levin

The right voluntarily to associate together as a military company or organization, or to drill or parade with arms, without and independent of an Act of Congress or law of the State authorizing the same, is not an attribute of national citizenship. Military organization and military parade under arms are subjects especially under the control of the government of every country. They cannot be claimed as a right independent of law. Under our political system they are subject to the regulation and control of the State and Federal Governments, acting in due regard to their respective prerogatives and powers. The Constitution and laws of the United States will be searched in vain for any support to the view that these are privileges and immunities of citizens of the United States independent of some specific legislation on the subject.

The United States Supreme Court
Presser v. Illinois (1886)

Foreword

Vigorous dissent is at the heart of our system of constitutionally guaranteed freedoms and democratic government. The right to follow one's own path, and to speak against popular sentiment and government action one opposes, is a fundamental right of every American upon which the framers of our Constitution lavished their every attention. The thread of dissent is so thoroughly woven into our law and into our everyday actions that it is easy to lose sight of just how much we freely and routinely disagree with each other.

When we look closely at virtually any aspect of daily life in America—whether it be how we worship, what our trade policy should be, or how best to address violent crime—it becomes immediately clear that Americans are capable of thoroughly disagreeing on just about everything. Not only do we disagree, we take vigorous advantage of an enormous range of means to express that disagreement. We register our dissent with each other in public forums, wage our battles at the polls, and push, pull, and prod our government to take actions that support our beliefs.

But until perhaps very recently, and taking pride in our diversity of peoples and ideas, we have managed, amid our differences, to forge the proudest system of self-rule in the world. Two conditions have enabled us to prevail: a good-faith effort among a majority of our citizens and legislators to make our nation the most free, tolerant, and peaceful nation on earth; and a common recognition in the wisdom and legitimacy of our Constitution as the basis for our laws, freedoms, and government.

Thus, it is with a sense of concern and uneasiness about the future of our democracy that I refer all Americans of good faith to a small but extraordinarily sinister development—the rise of armed paramilitary organizations, many of which are popularly known as militias—that threatens to undermine our laws, our freedoms, our safety, and our form of government. For these same reasons, I recommend to those Americans this very skilled analysis of the militia movement by two expert analysts: Thomas Halpern of the Anti-Defamation League, and Brian Levin of the Southern Poverty Law Center.

Let me be very careful here to describe exactly what I mean, and, in this way, reflect the precise but compelling analysis of the militia movement contained in this book. The First Amendment guarantees all Americans the right to peaceably assemble and to engage in heated debate critical of anyone and everything. It even guarantees the right to wear quirky military costumes and to give ourselves names that sound hostile and ominous. Whether a group calls itself the "knights" of one thing or the "militias" of another is of little moment. What matters is what a given group and its members do.

Many so-called militias are little more than oddly uniformed debating societies. While I might disagree with much of what they have to say, I do not quarrel with the right of that kind of militia to exist and the right of its members to advocate their views. These militias are not by any means the "well regulated militia" of the Constitution. But they are no threat to the Constitution. Their peaceable assemblies indeed reflect the Constitution's first premise of a right to free speech.

But there is another, very different kind of militia—armed paramilitary organizations that have grown up in the shadowy margins of political debate. For whatever twisted reasons—whether out of personal psychosis or hatred of fundamental human values—members of these groups have crossed a line that our society cannot tolerate. These militias have gone beyond peaceable assembly to overt preparation to engage in armed rebellion with guns, bombs, and even biological pathogens.

Although Congress has just begun to fulfill its duty to educate itself about militias, it is already clear that a hard core within this movement has crossed the line between vigorous debate and violent action. Incidents of violence, intimidation, and threats—often with clear links to hate philosophies such as white supremacy and neo-Nazism—are documented almost daily.

A curious aspect of these groups is the Alice-in-Wonderland nature of their political philosophy. Their "philosophies" often are little more than a bizarre pastiche of words and phrases appropriated from our Constitution and other organic and historic documents. But the meaning given to these words is twisted beyond all recognition. The political wisdom upon which all modern democracies are founded—our democracy most notably—is contorted by these groups into the service of hate and reaction.

The militias defend their hijacking of a reasoned and learned constitutionalism with the threat of violence against anyone and everyone with whom these groups disagree. Antigovernment rebellion is elevated to a constitutional duty, while the rest of us are demoted from citizens to co-conspirators or sheep foolishly compliant with tyrants. "Liberty" becomes the exclusive right of these groups and those who agree with them; including the "freedom" to violently attack the objects of their hate and animosity. At the extremes, their assessment of "rights" and their conception of government lead to the delegitimation of our Constitution and the process by which we govern ourselves.

What can a democratic society do to protect itself against such a violent and anarchistic movement? First, we must strengthen our criminal laws to ensure that violence and threats of violence are deterred, and appropriately punished when they occur. Nothing in our Constitution protects those who cross the line into violence, and we must deal sternly with those who do.

Second, and perhaps more importantly, we must deal with these groups in the long term by publicly exposing the sickness of their message. Their growth will be contained and their membership will wither when the tools of a free society—information and open debate—are used to expose the false premises of their constitutional doctrines, the error of their racist ideologies, and the danger to our society that their hatred breeds.

The work of Thomas Halpern and Brian Levin in *The Limits of Dissent* is an excellent contribution to that important effort of thoughtful and well-documented rebuttal. The two contributors, with assistance from Howard Friel of Aletheia Press, a skilled interlocutor, lay open the true anatomy of the armed civilian militia movement, and treat its status under our Constitution with scholarly care. As we almost routinely have come to expect, this book is another fine contribution to the fight against extremism from persons affiliated with the Anti-Defamation League and the Southern Poverty Law Center.

Of course, no one can stop persons of ill will from spouting whatever lies or distortions that may come into their minds. But this book will discredit the falsehoods on which the dark side of the militia movement justifies its existence. It is a solid shield of reason for persons of good will to raise against the forces of hate and violence in the United States.

Few things are more vital in America today than to engage
in the debate about these groups. I commend this book to every concerned citizen and serious scholar who wishes to join
in the important business of preserving the right to dissent,
while protecting our society against violent assault from within.

CHARLES E. SCHUMER
RANKING MEMBER,
SUBCOMMITTEE ON CRIME,
U.S. HOUSE OF REPRESENTATIVES

One

THE MILITIA MOVEMENT
Thomas Halpern

Aletheia Press: In October of 1994, the Anti-Defamation League (ADL) published its first report on the militia movement. As one of the coauthors, you wrote that "[b]ands of armed right-wing militants, most calling themselves 'militias,' are cropping up across America." You found evidence of their activity in no fewer than thirteen states, and expressed concern about the extremist and potentially violent nature of the movement. This report was issued several months before the bombing of the federal building in Oklahoma City on April 19, 1995.

In April of 1995, a few days before the bombing in Oklahoma City, the American Jewish Committee (AJC) issued its first report on the militia movement, stating: "In little over a year, since the coming to light of the Militias of Montana in February, 1994, a well-armed and dangerous antigovernment militia movement has been spreading with lightning pace across the country, 'preparing for war with the government.'" The AJC report estimated that militia groups were active in over thirty states.

Shortly after the bombing, ADL issued its second report on the militia movement in May, 1995, stating that "ADL surveys two weeks

131

after the Oklahoma City bombing indicated evidence of militia
activity in at least 32 states, with signs that the total number might
continue to rise."[3] One month later, in its third publication on the
militia movement, ADL reported "disturbing evidence that the militia
movement has continued to grow since the Oklahoma City bombing," and that "militias have been found to be operating in at least
40 states.[24]

And in June, 1995, Klanwatch, a project of the Southern Poverty Law Center, published a report on the militia movement stating
that "[a]t least 224 militias and their support groups ... are active
in 39 states.[25] Today, in early 1996, Klanwatch reports that there
are well over four hundred militia groups operating in the United
States, with militias now in every state.[6]

These reports, issued in an eighteen-month period, document
a rapid rate of growth in the militia movement. With this context
as our starting point, when did ADL first begin to notice the formation of the militia movement, which has emerged so suddenly
in this short period of time?

Thomas Halpern: At ADL we first became aware of the militia
issue I would say in the first half of 1994, when our national office began to pick up signals from a number of our regional offices and other sources around the country that small bands of armed
militants were forming. Many of these groups, though not all of
them, were calling themselves militias after the use of that term
in the Second Amendment of the U.S. Constitution.

One of the places where this was occurring was in the Pacific
Northwest; but there was militia organizing in other areas of the
country as well, in Michigan, for example. At first we were not
sure whether this was an isolated phenomenon in certain regions
of the country, nor were we sure about the potential for growth
and influence these early signs represented. But we continued to
watch the development of the movement, and we soon saw that it
was spreading to a number of different states around the country.

While there were differences among the various groups, we
noticed that there were common issues and themes on which the
militias were agitating. These issues were gun-control measures,

specifically the Brady bill and the ban on assault weapons, as well as two confrontations with federal law enforcement agencies: the siege involving the Branch Davidians in Waco, Texas, and the confrontation involving Randy Weaver in Ruby Ridge, Idaho. Organizing in response to these issues essentially marked the origins of the militia movement.

A.P. What was the special significance of Waco and Ruby Ridge and the gun-control bills to the origins of the militia movement?

T.H. From the beginning, the militias pointed to gun-control measures as precursors to overarching federal tyranny. In their view the federal government was steamrollering toward imposing tyranny on the American people, and the prerequisite for this happening would be a federal move to take away people's guns through gun-control legislation. In other words, gun control is seen by the militia movement as a Trojan Horse that would allow the government to confiscate everyone's guns and lay the groundwork for taking away people's liberties. The militias pointed to the incidents at Waco and Ruby Ridge as evidence that the federal government would stop at nothing to impose its tyrannical will on the American people.

From the militias' standpoint, the necessary response to federal tyranny is to stockpile weapons and engage in paramilitary training in preparation for what they regard as an impending showdown with the federal government. They exhibit their extreme hostility toward federal law enforcement agencies, most especially the Federal Bureau of Investigation (FBI) and the Bureau of Alcohol, Tobacco and Firearms (ATF). So the militias regard a showdown with the law enforcement agencies of the federal government as something that is clearly on the horizon, and a conflict they are going to be ready to engage in through paramilitary training and resistance.

A.P. When did you begin to suspect that the militia movement might not be an isolated phenomenon in a few parts of the country?

T.H. I was pretty sure of it by late summer in 1994. I was at a law enforcement conference, attended by federal, state, and local law enforcement personnel from across the country, to deliver a presentation on extremist groups of various kinds—neo-Nazi Skinheads, Ku Klux Klan, Nation of Islam, and others. At one point in my presentation, I stopped and noted that we were concerned about a more recent development, which was the formation of these militias. Quite a few of the officials in the room began to nod their heads, and we got into a discussion. Some of the conference attendees were more familiar than others with the militias. But that initial reaction was one of the clear indications that we were on to something; that the militias were a significant trend on the far right.

By fall 1994 this movement had spread, and it began to grow in different states around the country. So we in the Fact Finding Department at ADL decided that it was time for us to produce a report exposing the militias. We do not make such a decision lightly, by the way, especially when it comes to new movements. We want to feel sure that we are not overstating the threat from an extremist group that could fade out as quickly as it appeared, and that we are not giving undue attention and publicity that might help it attract additional membership or support.

The militias, though, if anything, appeared to be gaining momentum. So we asked our regional offices to gather as much information about them as they could, and we went public with our findings in October 1994, in the form of our first militia report, "Armed and Dangerous: Militias Take Aim at the Federal Government." We presented evidence of militia activity in thirteen states, and described the activities of the militia groups, their antidemocratic nature, and their challenge to the rule of law. The report did get some attention at the time, though this dissipated relatively soon after its release. But we continued to monitor the growth of the movement over the next several months.

It was, of course, the bombing of the federal building in Oklahoma City in April, 1995, that put the militia movement on the front pages across America, and which renewed intense interest in the movement among journalists, law enforcement, and the public. Within two months of Oklahoma City, as you mentioned, we issued a follow-up report on the militias, wherein we estimated that the militia movement had spread to forty states, and had grown to some fifteen thousand members. The evidence suggested that, despite the horror and revulsion at the bombing, the growth of militias overall continued after Oklahoma City. There were gains in some areas and losses in others, but the gains clearly appeared to outweigh the losses.

This growth in militia membership was due primarily to the overwhelming amount of publicity that the militias got in the wake of Oklahoma City—certainly an unintended consequence of the media coverage. The media obviously had a legitimate interest in these groups. But one consequence was to raise awareness of the existence of these militias among potential recruits and this, we felt, was a contributing factor in their growth. This is one of the consequences of living in a free society—a society whose freedoms, these militias claim ironically, have been irretrievably eroded.

A.P. The bombing of the federal building in Oklahoma City was the worst act of domestic terrorism in U.S. history, is that correct?

T.H. So far as I know, yes, that's right.

A.P. Nearly 170 innocent people were killed in the bombing, yet that incident inspired substantial growth in the militia movement. Does this fact gives us some insight into the nature of this movement? For example, much of the press coverage after the bombing focused on the extremist antigovernment ideology of the militias, which arguably provided the motivation for the bombing. The two suspects arrested for the bombing, Timothy McVeigh and Terry Nichols, were known to harbor extreme antigovernment views. And there are anti-Semitic and racist components to the militia movement as well, which were described in detail in press reports across the country. Because much of what we talk about today when we talk about the militias involves people who signed up after Oklahoma City, and after detailed press coverage of the antigovernment fanaticism, racism, and anti-Semitism that drives the movement, what does this say about the movement as it exists today?

T.H. There are a number of ways to get at that issue. It is important to understand that while there exists within the militia movement a strain of bigotry, and we have analyzed and reported on that, and I hope to elaborate a bit more on this aspect, the predominant extremist theme that runs through the movement is this exceptional hostility toward the federal government. It is the antigovernment hatred, rather than racial or religious bigotry, that has really driven the movement.

That being said, however, there does exist a strain of bigotry, particularly one of anti-Semitism within the movement, and we have continued to watch for growth in this anti-Semitic strain partly because the nature of conspiracy-mongering is that those who engage in it will often turn their sights on the Jews.

It also appears to me that some of the conspiracy ideas that militia members and activists promote may not name Jews directly, but reflect anti-Semitic views nevertheless—the use of terms like "international bankers," for example. I would say that the anti-Semitic strain can run from subtle to overt, and from a sort of semiconscious to a conscious anti-Semitism within the minds of some activists. So you do have a range. But I think that the main reason why some people have been attracted to the militia movement in the aftermath of the Oklahoma City bombing, just as before the bombing, had much more to do with the antigovernment feeling.

But your question about people signing up with the movement after the bombing leads to a problem that the movement faced: How would they reconcile the image of the government as oppressor with that of the victims of the bombing of a government building? And the answer that many militiamen rushed to was that the government did it. One of the themes we saw the militias hammer on again and again in the weeks following the bombing of the federal building was this outrageous notion that the federal government itself was responsible for what had happened—for bombing its own building and killing 169 people, including its own employees, the children of its employees, and others. In some sense, I think this was how those involved in the militia movement could justify to themselves their inclination to remain involved. They had been harping against the supposed evil of the federal government for so long and, lo and behold, someone came along and committed this despicable act against a federal target. If you can convince yourself that the government itself is responsible for the bombing, this gives you a certain ability to carry on with the antigovernment views that you have been expressing.

With the publicity that militia leaders and the militia movement were able to garner after the Oklahoma City bombing, they were able to reach that segment of the population that is susceptible to these kinds of antigovernment conspiracies. People who already had a deep suspicion of the federal government, and who were of the view that the federal government was overreaching in its authority, could be persuaded that the bombing was not merely the culmination of a series of acts by some violent individuals, but rather part of a larger government conspiracy. And this is consistent with the other conspiracy theories that drove the movement before the bombing, and that continue to drive it today.

If you look at the kind of reasoning that supports the notion that the U.S. government blew up its own building and its own people in Oklahoma City, this kind of reasoning also is behind the other antigovernment theories that are circulated among militia groups. They have spun a number of bizarre conspiracies, which in their view support the notion of the emergence of a tyrannical and conspiratorial federal government: the idea of black helicopters conducting surveillance on Americans across the country; the claim that concentration camps are being set up across the country to intern dissenters, including militia activists. These supposed concentration camps are being established, the conspiracy theorists say, by the Federal Emergency Management Agency (FEMA), the same federal agency, by the way, among other federal agencies, that did such heroic work in the wake of the Oklahoma City disaster.

Militia groups also claim that there are secret stencil markings on the back of road signs on interstate highways and other roads directing foreign troops. They believe that there are foreign troops mobilized in the United States, sometimes labeled United Nations or New World Order, which are prepared to subvert the United States as we know it, and which are in league with the federal government to accomplish this. They sometimes claim that foreign military equipment, often Russian military equipment, is prepositioned in this country to be used in this takeover, which is being planned by the federal government and the United Nations, as well as by the New World Order.

A.P. Could you clarify what the term "New World Order" means?

T.H. The New World Order is not, of course, an international organization or world body. The militias and their supporters use the term to refer to a shadowy global conspiracy that they say will strip Americans of our rights and reduce us virtually to slavery.

The term, New World Order was, in my understanding, essentially coined by political commentators to describe the condition that existed in international politics after the fall of Communism in Eastern Europe and the Soviet Union. For some it embodied hope, now that the Cold War was over, for a spirit of cooperation in international relations and problem-solving. But this descriptive label for the post–Communist situation in world politics has been seized by antigovernment extremists as proof in their minds of a diabolical global plot to take over the United States by the use of force.

One reason that this term holds such power for the militias is that former President George Bush used it a few years ago during the Persian Gulf crisis. The president was engaged in a difficult diplomatic effort to rally support from a number of reluctant partners for a multinational effort to turn back Iraqi aggression in Kuwait, and he was ultimately successful. The United States was in a position to assemble that alliance precisely because of the West's victory in the Cold War, which left the United States as the sole superpower. It seems, though, that what stuck in the minds of many militia proponents was a vision of the subordination of the United States to an international collective, resulting in the surrender of its national sovereignty and the stripping away of freedoms that Americans enjoy. It is a nightmare scenario that conjures up an

America defeated by international conspirators. It really stands the American victory in the Cold War on its head.

A.P. Many militia groups and individuals call themselves Constitutionalists or Patriots and, on a superficial level, this would seem to conflict with their hatred for the federal government. For example, while they call themselves Constitutionalists and Patriots, they refuse in many instances to recognize the authority of the federal government. This is apparently a conflict within their own model.

T.H. Quite so. The choice on their part of the term Patriot, for many of them, reflects a view of themselves, or an image that they wish to project to the public, that they are the inheritors of the tradition of the Revolutionary War patriots. Just as American patriots in the Revolutionary War period were fighting against the tyranny of the British Crown, so they, today, these so-called contemporary Patriots, are opposing the tyranny they see coming from the federal government of the United States. I think this is the sense in which the usage of the term has such meaning and resonance for them.

The description of militia members as Constitutionalists is worth looking into as well. These Constitutionalists are, by and large, people who take the responsibility of interpreting the Constitution into their own hands. Then they, or people who hang on their every word, may engage in conduct, based on these ad hoc interpretations, that violates existing law and existing constitutional interpretation and procedures. This perception among the militias that they are stand-alone and authoritative interpreters of the Constitution deliberately overlooks the fact that we have had a two-hundred-year tradition in this country of constitutional interpretation taking place within a sound judicial framework. The Constitution provides for a very sound system of government, and for the enactment, interpretation, and enforcement of laws that properly and lawfully guide our society. The Constitution provides a framework for bills to be enacted by the Congress, signed into law or vetoed by the President, and interpreted when necessary by the courts. The checks and balances that are built into this system of government, and the rights of the citizenry to free speech, to a free press, and to freely elect our representatives, provide us with the oversight to ensure that the government does not become a tyranny.

The members of the militia movement possess these rights just as fully as you and I do. I want to be very clear and very emphatic about that. However, the militias, while claiming to be Constitutionalists, tend to pick and choose those aspects of the Constitution which they approve or disapprove, and come up with all kinds of rationales and explanations and conspiracy theories which, in their view, prove that this portion of the Constitution is proper, or this one is improper or was never properly adopted, or is otherwise illegitimate for any of a number of bizarre reasons.

To some degree they can succeed in confusing potential recruits because the arguments that they make can sound reasonable or sophisticated to potential sympathizers, who may lack the kind of understanding that would enable them to see through the arguments made by these self-described Constitutionalists.

A.P. Can you give me a sense of the constitutional model put forward by the Constitutionalists among the militia movement?

T.H. Some constitutional arguments that militias put forward may be superficially persuasive, perhaps the one about gun rights and the Second Amendment, and even there the militias' claims are disputed by a great many legal scholars. For the most part, however, the constitutional interpretations of the militia movement are just not at all credible, and it is sometimes difficult to understand just how they acquire the following that they do. For example, people who support the proliferation of so-called common law courts in some areas of the country—a development that involves militias in some instances—state that they do not recognize the jurisdiction or constitutionality of the federal court system. They often make the absurd claim that the Constitution of the United States was suspended by the government years ago and was never restored, and common law court proponents may assert that the legitimacy of their own bogus courts derives from the Bible, the Magna Carta, the Declaration of Independence, and the Bill of Rights.

With regard to the Bill of Rights, which consists of the original ten amendments to the U.S. Constitution, some so-called Constitutionalists do not recognize the authority or legitimacy of the amendments to the Constitution enacted after the first ten.

A.P. So this would exclude the Thirteenth Amendment, which abolished slavery, the Fourteenth Amendment, which extended citizenship to freed slaves and provides equal protection under the laws to all citizens, the Sixteenth Amendment, which gives Congress the constitutional authority to tax personal incomes, and the Nineteenth Amendment, which gives women the right to vote.

T.H. It would, wouldn't it? In fact, a prominent militia leader recently drew up an ultimatum commanding Congress to initiate legislation to repeal the Fourteenth, Sixteenth, and Seventeenth Amendments, and the Brady bill and NAFTA.

Many of these notions help explain where the antigovernment fervor comes from, and they help explain why the militia movement views the federal government as a tyranny. If you think that the federal court system is unconstitutional, that the amendments enacted after 1791 are unconstitutional, and that the government does not have the constitutional right to enact gun-control laws and to collect income taxes, then you might view the government as a tyranny.

A.P. Can I ask you about this idea of federal tyranny? The United States is unique among industrialized countries in that it does not regulate certain conduct that other industrialized countries regulate. For example, the United States is the only industrialized country in the world that does not have a comprehensive federal gun-control law. Other industrialized countries regulate firearms possession and ownership in a manner that is much stricter than in the United States. This is the case even with the passage of the Brady bill and the assault weapons ban, which represent very modest restrictions on gun ownership. In the United States, the free speech rights of an individual are perhaps greater than in any other country. Most other industrialized countries prohibit the existence of private armies, such as the militias we have today in the United States. We have perhaps the lowest tax rate in comparison with other industrial nations. So when the militias talk about federal tyranny, notwithstanding their own interpretation of the Constitution, there is a paradox here because this country gives its citizens more formal rights and freedoms than any other government would give them.

T.H. My impression is that what they object to most is gun control, which they see as a violation of their perceived Second Amendment rights. However, although gun control is overwhelmingly the most important political issue that has animated the militias, a number of them have agitated over other issues that they also contend are signs that the federal government is increasingly imposing its will on the population—for example, in areas of the environment, education, and in some cases, abortion.

They also object to the direction in which they believe the country is moving in terms of government regulation, rather than an absolute standard of individual freedoms as contrasted to foreign countries. They perceive the United States to be less free than it was in the good ol' days. The militias reflect a general sense, present particularly in the western regions of the United States, that a man used to be able to stake out his piece of property, his homestead, to make a life for himself and his family, and do whatever he wanted to do virtually free of any kind of government oversight. In this respect the antigovernment posture of the militias is an extremist, nostalgic view of the way things used to be, and the way they should be today.

As time has passed, according to members of the militias and others with similar views, the government has become increasingly involved in every aspect of a normal person's life, and this is a process which, they say, is continuing and accelerating, and which is going to lead to government tyranny and an armed response from the militias if something is not done to stop it. In fact, in the introduction of our first militia report, there is a quote from Norman Olson of the Michigan Militia. Olson criticizes the direction in which the country and the government are headed, and describes what the militias plan to do in response: "We're talking about a situation where armed conflict may be inevitable if the country doesn't turn around."[7]

As for the comparison with other countries, it is my sense that many people who get involved in the militias are people who were not previously involved in political activity of any kind, and are not, by and large, people who have had much interest in comparative government. Their focus is on the United States and their own lives. In this context, however, I think there is a popular notion among Americans that the United States is a unique experiment regarding the extent of our individual freedoms, and I think that is actually true. But the militia extremists tend not to acknowledge that the freedoms contained in the Bill of Rights are not absolute. Americans are quite familiar with some of the exceptions to the right to free speech; for example, you cannot falsely shout "Fire" in a crowded theater. But when it comes to gun control, many militiamen are staunch in their view that the Second Amendment entitles them to have as many weapons or as much ammunition as they want, and of whatever type they want.

A.P. Would you like to talk about Waco and Ruby Ridge a bit more?

T.H. Those two events were critical to the genesis of the militia movement, mostly because they involved deadly confrontations over weapons-related issues—confrontations that were badly handled on the part of federal law enforcement agencies.

As we have seen from the various inquiries conducted by the Clinton administration and Congress into the handling of these two incidents, there is a great deal of concern over how the government dealt with those matters. Now it is one thing to say that the federal government and its law enforcement agencies badly managed those two crises, and that we should try to prevent such incidents in the future by looking at legislative or other remedies, such as tightening the rules of engagement, implementing stricter oversight, and so forth. But it is quite another thing to say, as the militias have said, that these episodes are evidence of the impending federal tyranny and of a federal government that would stop at nothing to impose its will upon the people.

Because gun control is the paramount political issue driving the militias, and because the confrontations at Waco and Ruby Ridge occurred due to alleged weapons-related crimes, these two incidents resonated a great deal with the militias. The militias regard gun control as a prelude to a complete trampling of constitutional rights by governmental authorities, and guns were at the very heart of the confrontations at both Waco and Ruby Ridge.

Another thing about the Branch Davidian controversy: Much of what we have seen concerning the militia view about Waco has emphasized the religious aspect of the Branch Davidian compound, and there seems to have been a serious attempt on the part of many militia advocates to characterize the siege of the compound as a particularly egregious act because the government had invaded the space of a religious community. This notion of the government's motivation ignores the very serious allegations concerning weapons violations that were leveled against David Koresh and the Branch Davidians, and instead focuses exclusively on allegations of violations of religious freedom—a subject that might evoke some sympathy among the American people.

A.P. Why do the militias view very modest restrictions on gun ownership, such as the Brady law and the assault weapons ban, as a threat to their security as individual citizens requiring, in their minds, an armed collective response? Essentially the Brady law provides for a waiting period and background check to prevent convicted felons from purchasing handguns, and the assault weapons ban outlaws the sale and purchase of certain classes of assault weapons.

Presumably, reasonable people would conclude that it is not a good idea to have convicted felons purchasing handguns. And, to my knowledge, the assault weapons ban was not even retroactive in its application. In other words, any militia member who legally purchased an assault weapon before the effective date of the ban is in lawful possession of the assault weapon. Again, this speaks to the modest sweep of the law. So why, within the militia cosmology, are the Brady law and the assault weapons ban such apocalyptic events?

T.H. As we have discussed, it is widely held within the militia movement that any gun-control law is in conflict with the Second Amendment because it interferes with the unfettered and absolute right of any and all U.S. citizens to purchase any firearm and any number of firearms of their choice, and that any violation of this right is a slippery slope to government tyranny. Not only is this absolutist stance rejected by many experts in constitutional law, it is also bound to clash with government efforts to protect its citizens from the threat of gun violence.

The militia hysteria over the Brady bill is an example of this clash. I have read that the principal purpose of the waiting period and the background check in the Brady bill was to provide a means of enforcement for a provision already existing in federal law that prohibited sales of handguns to people who had been convicted of a felony. Before the Brady bill was enacted into law, the ban on purchases by felons was enforced only by voluntary measures at the point of sale; there was no waiting period or background check in place to give the legitimate firearms dealer or governmental authorities an opportunity to verify that a purchaser had no felony record. Clearly, the government has an interest in keeping firearms out of the hands of convicted felons, as well as in enforcing laws designed to do this. Even the National Rifle Association, though it opposed the Brady bill, has supported in the past the idea of keeping firearms out of the hands of felons. Despite the Brady bill's narrowly-focused intent, the militias viewed the bill as bringing us to the edge of the apocalypse.

The other gun-control bill that served as a rallying cry for the militia movement was the ban on nineteen different types of assault weapons. This ban was part of the federal crime bill that was signed into law in 1994 by President Clinton. Assault weapons were the focus of the ban because they are antipersonnel weapons, the weapon of choice for drug dealers and gangs, and a serious threat to law enforcement.

Assault weapons also have been used in a number of multiple murders that have taken place across the country in recent years. For example, one of the events that prompted serious consideration of a ban on assault weapons was the random shooting with an assault weapon of a school yard full of children in Stockton, California in 1989. Five school children were killed in that incident, and many others were wounded.

A.P. If we look at these gun-control laws—the Brady law and the assault weapons ban—and what they do to protect public safety, and if we look at the holes in our firearms regulations that these measures were designed to patch, we can see two things: these gun laws were modest but very reasonable attempts by the government to protect public safety; and there is little reason or justification for the kind of antigovernment hysteria that these laws have brought about in the militia movement.

T.H. But in the view of militia propagandists, these laws were only the beginning. These gun-control measures, modest as they are in reality, are viewed by militia activists as the first step toward an eventual wholesale ban on private firearm ownership in this country. And that is the line they have been feeding to potential recruits and that has contributed to spurring this movement on.

If one is inclined toward a conspiracy view of the federal government, then almost any conspiracy scenario presented by the militias would be difficult to refute. This is because the argument will always be, regardless of how sensible or limited a gun-control law might be, that this particular gun law is only a first step toward ultimate confiscation, a precursor to a more foreboding endgame.

A.P. To what extent are gun shows important to the militia movement?

T.H. Gun shows play a role to the extent that they serve as a distribution point for militia propaganda, and as an occasional forum for speakers who advance a pro-militia line or antigovernment rhetoric that is consistent with the militia message. And militia groups and ordinary citizens alike may use gun shows as purchasing points for picking up weapons or ammunition or other kinds of material that they may then be stockpiling. There have been reports quoting militiamen and like-minded folks saying that they have seen gun salesmen or gun vendors coming to gun shows with two hundred cases of ammunition, and by the end of the weekend it is all gone. And stockpiling weapons and ammunition is consistent with advice that some militia leaders have given to the movement.

It is important to note that not everyone who goes to a gun show is going there to imbibe a radical antigovernment message or to join a militia group. But gun shows have undergone a significant change of character and function in recent years. My impression, and the impression of some others who have looked at this movement, is that a number of years ago these gun shows were not very political at all; they were primarily for gun collectors and firearms enthusiasts who were not particularly politically oriented. But more recently, in the last couple of years, gun shows have become much more politicized, to the extent that militia groups and other antigovernment activists regard them as potentially fruitful recruiting points and as efficient venues for spreading their message to those they believe are likely to be receptive to that message.

A.P. What is the extent, in your view, of the threat to civil order and democratic institutions that the militia movement poses?

T.H. One way to gauge the threat this movement poses is to look at what some groups or individuals within this movement have already done. There is a track record of violence in this movement in many states across the country. And there have been instances where militia groups have been found to be planning the use of force, particularly against government officials or institutions.

One example is the Blue Ridge Hunt Club, a militia group from Virginia. Members of this group were found to be stockpiling weapons, and one of them had a computer disk that contained a draft of the group's newsletter stating that the group planned to carry out terrorist actions against infrastructure facilities and to eliminate its enemies if need be.

There also have been examples of confrontations between militiamen and individual law enforcement officers that have been more spontaneous and that have resulted in violence. For example, in Ohio a militiaman was driving with homemade or phony license plates that were not regulation plates issued by the state of Ohio. The plate, which looked something like a real license plate but was still distinguishable from regulation Ohio tags, said MILITIA CHAPLAIN or something to this effect. A police officer pulled over the car bearing this homemade plate. According to the officer, the driver got out of the car with a gun in hand, and made a move toward the officer, who felt compelled to fire at the militiaman in self-defense. The militiaman was killed in this confrontation. A grand jury looked into this matter and decided that the evidence did not warrant bringing any charges against the officer.

No one wants to see injury or loss of life from situations like this one. But it is hard not to worry that it could happen, especially considering that some militiamen may bring to such a situation an already ingrained feeling that law enforcement is the enemy.

One of the dangers that we see from this movement is the potential for violence that can come from people who are inspired by the propaganda emanating from the movement. The kind of confrontation with law enforcement that I just described is the result in part of the kind of antigovernment hysteria that these militias pump out continuously. This hysteria induces paranoia among certain people in the movement or on its fringes.

The kind of extremist rhetoric that militias engage in may prompt the consumers of this information to take this message to heart, to hunker down in a siege mentality, either at home or while out and among the public. This can create a potentially explosive situation when, for example, a police officer attempts to deal with a minor traffic violation. If an individual believes that he or she is a "sovereign" citizen and not subject to federal and state law, as a number of antigovernment extremists believe, then an attempt by a police officer to enforce even traffic laws can lead to a potentially violent or even fatal encounter. This was apparently the case in the incident involving the license plate in Ohio marked MILITIA CHAPLAIN.

There are people out there combining firearms and paramilitary training with ideas about the illegitimacy of established law and government, and that is a highly combustible mixture. The potential for violence in this kind of setting is very high, and small groups of people, or even lone individuals, may be driven to commit acts of violence. One of the lessons of the Oklahoma City bombing last April is that it does not take a mass movement to commit acts of tremendous horror.

A.P. Is there evidence of militia groups organizing as leaderless cells? If so, could you explain what these are?

T.H. There is evidence that militia groups are organizing themselves in this fashion. The concept of leaderless resistance dates back more than thirty years, and was originally articulated in the context of organizing cells that would be equipped for armed resistance in the event of a communist takeover of the United States. More recently, though, leaderless resistance has been pushed by a number of far-right figures, including neo-Nazis, as a tactic in their battle against the federal government. The idea in summary is, rather than organizing a group in a structure that has members, a group hierarchy, and a leader that can be easily detected, resisters would organize themselves into small cells of from three to five or so individuals, and strike at targets of their own choosing at times of their own choosing. The presumed benefits are that these small cells will be much less prone to detection or infiltration by law enforcement or others, and that it will be very difficult to show that movement leaders are legally responsible for crimes committed by their followers, as has been shown in civil lawsuits against such hate groups as the White Aryan Resistance and factions of the Ku Klux Klan. Our investigations have shown that there are people who have been encouraging militia groups to organize themselves along these lines.

A.P. Could an analogy be drawn between the leaderless resistance cells and an armed underground?

T.H. Yes, that is what they are. They are underground rather than above ground, and some are heavily armed in the way that many of the militia groups are armed. The responsibility of law enforcement to protect the public from the danger represented by these leaderless cells is very difficult to carry out when they organize themselves in this secret and underground fashion. The irony is, if the government were as tyrannical as some of the militia advocates say it is, and were as all-powerful, there would not be much difficulty for law enforcement to detect and counteract these armed underground units.

One of the obstacles law enforcement faces in seeking to protect the public from these leaderless cells has to do with the fact that law enforcement cannot act against them just because they are secretive, or if they are not engaged in criminal activity. But this is where the paramilitary training statutes come into play, which many states have already enacted. If evidence can be developed, and this is not always an easy thing, that these groups are engaging in paramilitary training with the intent to create a civil disorder, then laws banning paramilitary training can be exercised to counteract these activities.

These anti-paramilitary training laws target those who teach or demonstrate to others, or who receive instruction, about the use, application, or making of firearms, explosives, or incendiary devices, intending or knowing that these training methods would be unlawfully employed in the furtherance of a civil disorder. These laws have been enacted in roughly half the states of the union, many of them based on an ADL model statute.

There is also a federal statute that addresses those who teach or demonstrate this kind of training with the same intent. However, the federal law currently in force does not cover those who receive training in paramilitary activities. It is important on both the state and federal levels to enact laws punishing those who gather to receive paramilitary instruction, as well as those who provide the instruction.

A.P. In recent years, there has been a growing insurgency of antigovernment, right-wing militia and extremist groups in the

United States, many with an inclination to heavily arm themselves. Is there a modern historical precedent in the United States for the armed civilian militias and their antigovernment ideology?

T.H. We at ADL perceived early on, when we began to notice signs of the development of the militias, that their antigovernment views were reminiscent of other extremist groups from the 1970s and 1980s. These earlier groups were overtly racist and anti-Semitic. In the militia movement, too, we have observed racism and anti-Semitism, in addition to hatred of the government.

One of the first things that caught our attention about the militias was the coupling of an intense hostility to the federal government and an occasional expression of support by a militiaman for the local sheriff. This reminded us of the Posse Comitatus, a group whose heyday was in the early to mid-1980s. The Posse, whose name is Latin for "power of the county," was a virulently anti-Semitic and antigovernment group who believed that there was no legitimate governmental authority above the county level. Accordingly, Posse members often refused to pay taxes, refused to get driver's licenses, and refused to operate vehicles with license plates. Some Posse members got involved in some very serious violent episodes with law enforcement. The most well-known example is the case of Gordon Kahl.

Kahl was a North Dakota farmer and Posse member. In 1983, after a conviction for nonpayment of taxes, Kahl killed two federal marshals who came to arrest him for violating his parole. Kahl avoided arrest and became a fugitive. He died some time later in a shoot-out with law enforcement agents in Arkansas, during which a sheriff was killed. As a result of this incident, Gordon Kahl became a martyr to the far right, and videos about his story are offered for sale in the militia movement and by others on the far right.

In addition to being antigovernment, as I mentioned earlier, the Posse Comitatus was also deeply anti-Semitic. Posse activists followed the pseudo-religious tenets of the Christian Identity movement, which declares Jews to be the children of Satan, blacks and other nonwhite races to be subhuman "mud people," and northern European whites to be the "chosen people" of the Bible. The claim by Posse activists that all legitimate government authority is rooted at the county level conforms with their view that the federal and state governments are controlled by enemies of the white race, and these enemies are usually identified as Jews. So their hostility to the federal government flows from their anti-Semitism.

In an ADL report released shortly after the Oklahoma City bombing, we described the Posse Comitatus and some of these far-right precursors to the militia movement, such as the Committee of the States, The Order, and the Aryan Nations, a group that still exists today. I thought that I would share with you brief excerpts from that report, to convey the antigovernment as well as the anti-Semitic and racist nature of these groups.

Here are excerpts from our report on a group called the Committee of the States:

> The Committee of the States was a right-wing extremist tax protest group that was formed on July 4, 1984, in Mariposa, California. William Potter Gale, a long-time anti-Jewish activist associated with the Posse Comitatus and the [Christian] Identity movement, and "Pastor" of his own Identity church, was instrumental in its founding. Aryan Nations founder Richard G. Butler also signed the document that formed the group.
>
> The Committee of the States took its name from the Articles of Confederation, predecessor to the U.S. Constitution, which called for a committee of the states to run the nation. The group initially came to public attention by way of a 1985 article in the *Los Angeles Daily Journal*, which stated that the committee had a stronghold of some 25 supporters in the area of Sacramento, California, and participants in Nevada, Idaho, Iowa and Wisconsin. The article outlined some of the group's beliefs:
>
>> They subscribed to the theory of the extremist group Posse Comitatus that the highest legal authority should lie with the counties and county sheriffs, and in citizen

grand juries. They opposed government regulation of any kind, especially the federal income tax.

They contended that the courts are functioning under martial law, an "admiralty jurisdiction" which was opposed by the nation's founding fathers. They claim such laws favor merchants and the banks, and that the federal government and international bankers are enslaving Americans with the aim of a Communist takeover.

They held that God's law as proclaimed in the Bible takes precedence over man-made law. Some Committee of the States members turned in their driver's licenses and removed the license plates from their cars to demonstrate their opposition to such governmental regulations.[8]

The following is part of what we reported on the Aryan Nations:

Aryan Nations militantly advocates anti-Semitism and the establishment of a white racist state. Although primarily an Identity group, [Richard] Butler's Aryan Nations reflects a Nazi-like philosophy; Butler himself has praised Hitler. During the 1980s, several of Butler's followers joined members of the neo-Nazi National Alliance and some KKK splinter groups to form a secret organization known as The Order, which planned to overthrow the U.S. government. To raise money for their planned revolution, The Order engaged in a crime spree involving murder, counterfeiting, bank robberies and armored car hold-ups....

Aryan Nations has been mentioned prominently in connection with one of the incidents that militia groups cite as evidence of a government conspiracy against the citizenry—the 1992 Randy Weaver confrontation in northern Idaho. Weaver, a white supremacist who had reportedly visited the Aryan Nations compound in the past, resisted an effort by federal agents to arrest him at his remote cabin for alleged weapons violations. Weaver's wife and son were killed during the stand-off, along with a deputy U.S. marshal. During the siege, groups of Aryan Nations supporters, in addition to Skinheads and other neo-Nazis, rallied in support of Weaver near his cabin.[9]

Concerning The Order, the revolutionary neo-Nazi gang that murdered Denver talk-radio host Alan Berg and committed numerous other crimes, I would add that it borrowed many of its terrorist plans from the pages of a novel called *The Turner Diaries*. This novel, written by an American neo-Nazi leader named William Pierce, was reportedly a favorite of Timothy McVeigh, one of the Oklahoma City bombing suspects, and it contains a fictional account of the destruction of the FBI building in Washington by an ammonium nitrate and fuel oil bomb that is very similar to the actual bombing of the federal building in Oklahoma City.

The groups whose descriptions I have provided here are relevant to this discussion because they and others are among the far-right groups that can be considered precursors to the militias. I have emphasized that while a strain of anti-Semitism exists in the militia movement, it is not universal; but the fierce hatred of the federal government that characterizes the militias is very much in tune with the antigovernment hatred expressed by the Posse Comitatus, by The Order, and by other far-right groups active in the 1970s and 1980s.

I should also note the influence of organizations that specialize in the dissemination of the kind of propaganda that we sometimes see in militia circles. For example, the Liberty Lobby—the anti-Semitic propaganda organization based in Washington, D.C.—is the leading anti-Semitic organization in America. It often dresses up its anti-Semitism in a guise of patriotism and populism, and it clearly saw in the militia movement, as the movement began to grow, an opportunity to reach new readers through its publication, *The Spotlight*.

In our ADL investigations of the militia movement, again and again we came across militia activists who said that they got their news from *The Spotlight,* and we also found militia-oriented materials enthusiastically endorsing *The Spotlight* as recommended reading. In this way, we feel that anti-Semitic groups have been able to influence, to a degree at least, the course of the militia movement.

Another interesting thing about the Liberty Lobby is that Timothy McVeigh was shown to have an interest in *The Spotlight.* The ADL revealed that he took out classified ads in *The Spotlight* in 1993, when he advertised replicas of light anti-tank weapon launchers as well as flares that could be launched from them and that could be modified for explosive use. This was in combination with McVeigh's activity on the gun-show circuit. In essence, then, by advertising his wares in *The Spotlight,* McVeigh was offering to arm any bigot, any anti-Semite, and any extremist in America, because *The Spotlight* is the most widely distributed publication in those extremist circles.

Another publication that is circulated in some militia circles is the *Protocols of the Elders of Zion,* a notorious czarist forgery purporting to be a blueprint for Jewish domination of the world. It is a seminal work of anti-Semitism, and has long been discredited. But it continues to crop up and feed anti-Semitic conspiracy views, and not only among right-wing extremists.

A.P. Would you say that the racism and anti-Semitism prevalent among the racist groups we have been discussing is a principal ideological component of the militia movement?

T.H. I would not go that far. It is important to remember that some militia groups have publicly gone to considerable lengths to distance themselves from racist and anti-Semitic views. Other militia groups might be more attracted to this kind of material. The key thing to underscore about the militias is that the movement is not monolithic. There is a continuum of beliefs and commitments, and racism and anti-Semitism do not characterize the entire movement.

A.P. On the other hand, indulging in antigovernment conspiracies clearly plays an important role in motivating the militia membership, as it did in the precursor movements. Many of these conspiracies involve depictions of sinister plots of the federal government, including, for example, the alleged building of concentration camps or plans to confiscate people's guns.

T.H. Some of these conspiracy scenarios do play an important role in recruiting new members. If you believe that the government is building concentration camps, you naturally are frightened of that prospect and probably want to do something about it. And once a person is in the conspiracy mindset, membership in a militia is a sensible answer from that perspective. As I have said before, the idea that the government is engaged in this massive conspiracy to deprive Americans of their rights, beginning with gun rights, leads many militias to believe in the necessity for paramilitary resistance, or at least paramilitary training.

A.P. Most people living in the United Sates have grievances with the federal government on some level or other. However, that people have grievances against the government, real or imagined, does not give them the right to initiate paramilitary training, form private armies, threaten federal officials and agencies with violence, or otherwise engage in illegal activities. Nor do these activities enjoy protected status under the Constitution. People with grievances against the government are not entitled under the Constitution to organize and train as private armies, and in many states to do so is illegal.

T.H. Correct. None of the fears they express gives them the right to resist laws properly enacted. No one has that right. This is how, and why, the rule of law and democracy work. This is one reason why we describe this extremist movement as antidemocratic, because the speech and conduct that we see in this movement certainly seem to encourage the idea that you can resist properly enacted laws through the use or threat of force.

A.P. Are there any other antigovernment grievances worth mentioning? There seems to be a common hostility toward the United Nations.

T.H. We frequently see references to the United Nations as an instrument through which the U.S. government collaborates with the New World Order to subvert American democracy and impose this shadowy tyranny over the people. References abound to New World Order or United Nations forces that will be the instrument to physically effect this armed takeover of America. In this regard, we have seen references to transport of foreign military equipment and United Nations military equipment within U.S. borders for purposes of an armed takeover of the country. Some militias charge that concentration camps are being set up by government agencies such as FEMA. We have seen charges that the foreign troops which supposedly are going to be effecting the takeover by the New World Order will be directed to the FEMA concentration camps by secret stencil markings on the backs of road signs.

A.P. What are those markings, do you know?

T.H. Somewhere I read a very sensible explanation from a fellow who I think was in some state department of transportation. It was something about how the markings indicate the age of the signs, because the letters lose their reflective quality after a number of years and need to be replaced. Probably any state transportation agency can give you the explanation you need.

At any rate, this is the stuff of militia fantasies. We also have seen militia proponents claiming that the federal crime bill was passed to authorize the hiring of one hundred thousand Royal Hong Kong police to begin implementing the New World Order with measures such as taking away people's guns. As is often the case with these conspiracy theories, there is the smallest grain of truth to the allegation from which is spun an incredible fiction.

My recollection about the Royal Hong Kong police—I do not think it was ever in any of the bills under consideration—but early on in a discussion of some crime bill over the past few years, there was a recognition of the impending return of Hong Kong from the British to the Communist Chinese, and a recognition that perhaps there might be some opportunity to utilize, perhaps for training purposes, the expertise of some highly-trained and professional police from Hong Kong. It never went anywhere, but that was likely the genesis of what became a nightmare scenario that caught on with some militias about Hong Kong police serving as the enforcers of a gun ban in America and a New World Order takeover of this country.

A.P. Regarding this fear of a United Nations, New World Order, or foreign troop takeover of the United States, again, we have this paradoxical situation where, with the exception of the threat of nuclear weapons, we live in the most secure country in the world. The United States is a country that is bordered to the east and west by two oceans, and to the north and south by friendly neighbors. We have by far the most powerful armed forces in the world. Yet, at the same time, the militia movement has this idea that the United States is ripe for a foreign takeover by forces ranging from Russian troops to the Royal Hong Kong police.

T.H. Ah, yes—which means, the conspiracy theorists would tell you, that the takeover can only succeed if it is approved and acquiesced in by the United States government. That gets at the heart of the question and the efficacy of these conspiracies. It is not that the U.S. government is prepared to use all of its unparalleled military might to repel this supposed invasion, but that the government is actually behind the invasion.

A.P. Perhaps this is where the so-called traitor files come from, where certain militia groups charge that Bill and Hillary Clinton are part of a Marxist terrorist takeover of the United States. To postulate that the United States is on the verge of an armed takeover by foreign troops, with the complicity of the federal government, necessarily entails...

T.H. It entails a conspiracy. Conspiracies abound in this movement, and there may be any variety of conspiracy theories that could pretend to explain how the United Nations or New World Order takeover is to occur. That is in part how conspiracy mongers operate. You can dream up anything you like; you are not bound by rules of reality.

Conspiracy theorists, for example, often grab at what they see in the headlines: GATT and NAFTA—perhaps spooky-sounding acronyms enter into it. Who knows? Once you believe that the federal government is on this course, you can find that almost anything is related to the conspiracy.

A.P. What is the geographic makeup of the militia movement?

T.H. I think that it must be said and understood that the militia movement still represents a small segment of the overall population. Even despite its rapid growth, which you sketched earlier, we are not talking about a mass movement. It is an extremist movement, and its adherents represent a tiny fraction of the American public. Even so, there is a greater number of people, impossible to estimate, who share some of the views of the militia movement. But I think that part of the appeal for those who have been attracted to the militias comes from certain aspects of their circumstances.

Although militias are present in every region of the country, militias did find some of their early momentum in the West and parts of the Midwest, largely in rural areas where feelings run high with regard to a perception that a distant federal bureaucracy in far-off Washington D.C. does not understand their lives, does not understand their problems, does not care about their lives or problems, and is simply bent on controlling how they go about living and working and earning a living and so forth.

The militias, of course, have protested and focused most intently on the question of gun control. Guns are part of the way of life in many areas of the country, and I think the controversy over gun control reflects the complexity and range of lifestyles in our country. Part of what is really unfortunate about this conflict over gun control, from the perspective of responsible citizens who support stricter gun laws, is that regulation of gun ownership is primarily a response to the problem of violent crime in the United States, mainly in the larger cities. Gun control represents an attempt to get a handle on a very serious problem facing our urban areas, where people lead very different lives from those who live in more rural areas. I think there has been a very deep gulf in understanding between the prototypical citizens on either side of this sociological divide. But the gun-control bills that have been enacted into law, and those that have been introduced and that have not been enacted into law to date, have tried to take into account the different requirements and lifestyles of our citizens who live in more rural areas. This fact has been lost amidst the din of opposition to gun-control bills that have been introduced.

A.P. In addition to opposition to gun control and the conspiracy mentality that we have discussed, are there other issues, perhaps relating to the economy and the decline in good jobs, that account for the growth of the militia movement? Is one of the scenarios for the growth of the militia movement a problematic industrial policy? Recently, the industrial base of our economy has eroded, and there has been a decline in manufacturing jobs which have been replaced largely by low-paying service jobs. For working class people—and much of the militia movement is comprised of working class people—the good jobs that used to be there are not there anymore. In the West, we have dwindling resources, and the clash between jobs on one hand and resource scarcity and environmental protection on the other has resulted in people losing jobs and ways of life that have been in families and communities for generations.

Does the loss of good jobs and traditional ways of life have anything to do with the rise of the militias?

T.H. I do not think the evidence supports the idea that a decline in manufacturing jobs contributed to the growth of the militia movement. It is not impossible, but the evidence for it is not there. Most of what the militias talk about has little to do with economic or industrial policies. What they say is so focused on these political questions and on what they claim are constitutional questions. While there are occasional references to things like NAFTA and GATT, they are presented as evidence of the deterioration of American sovereignty. In this area, the principal question is sovereignty, not whether there are economic pluses or minuses.

On the other hand, some militias from the beginning emphasized other areas, in addition to the core issue of gun control, in which they sought to turn back the clock on federal involvement. One such area was environmental regulation, which you mentioned in your question. The militia line was that environmental rules and regulations passed and implemented by Washington not only represented unfair encroachment by the government on the ability of Americans to use their land for whatever purposes they choose, but were also one more aspect of a runaway federal train destined for totalitarian rule and complete control of the lives of the people. This shows the way in which militia activists could tailor their message based on their perception of a particular audience.

A.P. To the best of your knowledge, what was the extent of the connection between the two suspects in the bombing of the federal building in Oklahoma City—Timothy McVeigh and Terry Nichols—to the militia movement or specific militia groups? Were these individuals members of a militia group or otherwise influenced by militia ideology?

T.H. We have always been careful to portray as accurately as we could, based on the available evidence, the relationship between the Oklahoma City bombing suspects and the militia movement, and there have been a number of accounts from reliable news organizations that place McVeigh and Nichols at some meetings of militia groups in Michigan. These accounts included statements from eyewitnesses. But beyond that, the extent of their involvement with the militias is not certain. I think it is valid and important to point out that the motivation that allegedly drove these suspects to bomb the building dovetails to a considerable degree with the driving forces of the militia movement, especially the fury over Waco. But the militia movement is of concern on its own merits, even apart from whatever degree of involvement the Oklahoma City bombing suspects may have had with the movement.

A.P. What are common law courts? There have been many reports in recent months about common law courts springing up in certain areas of the country. And you have mentioned them here.

T.H. Common law courts are bogus courts that function in defiance of the authority of real courts. To date, the antigovernment fervor of the recent period has been expressed in its most extreme form in the proliferation of militias engaging in paramilitary activities and in the threat of terrorism from other antigovernment zealots. Now it seems that there is also a proliferation of these common law courts. These fraudulent courts are of a similar extremist character, the attitude being not to slim down the government, but to take a match to it.

Participants in these common law courts regard the real courts as illegitimate on grounds that are difficult to fathom. Essentially, they claim a legitimacy for their courts, not just from the Constitution, but from the Magna Carta, from their reading of common law, and even from the Bible.

Some of these self-styled courts have tried to file official-looking but bogus documents with court clerks and other government officials. In extreme cases some of these courts—and I would use the word courts in quotation marks when referring to common law courts—some of these courts reportedly have charged government officials with treason or other crimes, and have even threatened the death penalty.

There is some overlap in participation between militia groups and common law courts, and there are common law courts that appear to operate apart from any militia connection. And just as we see with the militia groups, there are people playing leadership roles in the common law courts who have longer histories of participation in extremist movements. In the broader rank and file of both the militias and the common law courts, there is less extremism, but these are people who have been drawn into these movements because of their own frustrations, and who have been persuaded of the evils of the federal government. I think that there are people participating in these courts who have had difficulties in the real courts, and who have latched on to this movement as a way of seeking redress from what they regard as injustices that have been perpetrated on them by the legitimate judicial system. But their participation contributes to the growth of a movement that represents a very serious potential threat to our judicial system and to law and order, especially if common law courts defy the authorities and attempt to enforce their rulings. Some have indicated that they may use the militia for that very purpose.

A.P. At one point we were talking informally about the militias, and you mentioned that you thought the militias might be deemphasizing their military activity and reemphasizing their political activity? Could you explain what you meant by that?

T.H. There are some indications that, partly for public relations reasons in the wake of the Oklahoma City bombing, some militia groups are placing less of an emphasis on paramilitary-type activities, and more of an emphasis on political-type activities. For example, some militia groups have raised the possibility of working to place initiatives addressing issues of concern to them on ballots in their areas. Other groups have talked about other ways of engaging the political process in a way that remains anathema to other militia groups, who scoff at the idea of participation in the political process. For these more cynical militia members, participation on any level is simply buying into that corrupt process.

But many militias may not even follow through with these ideas, which have only been rather sketchily articulated. Even if they do, they may find that actual political work is sometimes hard work indeed. It takes organizing, knocking on doors, filing petitions, the kind of work that has frustrated long-time political professionals as well. It is quite possible that they will become easily frustrated and further persuaded that these are rules designed only to be obstacles to ordinary people expressing themselves. In other words, talk of greater participation in the political process could be short-lived, and could revert to the situation as it was before. And much of it has been for public relations value only.

Some militia leaders have scorned those who have even raised the idea of becoming more politically engaged, noting that this political activity has brought in moderates. They prefer pursuing a more hard-line agenda which involves, among other things, staying well clear of the political arena.

Two

MILITIAS AND THE CONSTITUTION
BRIAN LEVIN

Aletheia Press: Most of what we will discuss in this chapter involves the legal and constitutional issues that the militia movement causes us to consider. But there are some facts and definitional issues that I would like to sort out first. For example, I have come across these different qualifications for the word militia: "well-regulated militia," "state militia," "unorganized militia," and "sedentary militia"; none of which, to my knowledge, refer to the armed civilian militias that have been growing in numbers around the country as part of a larger antigovernment movement.

Could we begin by defining these terms and sorting out which ones are relevant to our discussion?

Brian Levin: These terms have a legitimate legal history that explains their existence and function, but they do not refer to the armed civilian militias that are currently committing and threatening acts of violence in parts of the country. These civilian militias have no legitimacy in the law.

So let me give you both a short answer and a long answer to your question: the short one to briefly identify these terms; the long one to give you a bit more explanation and history.

The "well-regulated militia" is the militia referenced in the Second Amendment and Militia Clauses of the U.S. Constitution. Today, this well-regulated militia is the National Guard of each of the fifty states, not the armed civilian militias.

The "state militia" refers to the militia that existed in each state in the eighteenth and nineteenth centuries under the Constitution as regulated armed units. Today, pursuant to federal legislation passed in 1903 known as the Dick Act,[1] the state militias are the National Guard of the fifty states. Thus, well-regulated militia, state militia, and the National Guard are more or less synonymous terms because they refer to the same thing, though labeled differently to reflect the historical and legal contexts in which they are used.

The "unorganized militia" also was established by the Dick Act, and is composed of able-bodied males between the ages of eighteen and forty-five. It constitutes a reserve pool of private citizens in the event that the government would require its use during extraordinary circumstances. This statute says that all able-bodied male citizens who fulfill the age requirement, and who are not serving in the armed forces of the United States or the National Guard, are members of the unorganized militia in their respective states. In other words, you and I are subject by this statute to be called into military service if and when our political representatives find it necessary. But this is the only obligation, privilege, right, or duty that you and I have under this law.

Contrary to what many militia groups maintain, this federal statute, and similar state statutes, do not give you and me the legal right to go out and form our own private armed militia, and it has never been interpreted by the courts to provide any private U.S. citizen with a right to organize, establish, or maintain a private militia or to conduct paramilitary training.

The "sedentary militia" is another term that is used to refer to the unorganized militia that I just described.

So these different labels essentially describe two separate kinds of militias that are established under federal law: (a) the well-regulated state militia established by the Constitution, which, pursuant to federal legislation, is now the National Guard, and (b) the unorganized or sedentary militia established by federal law. Neither one bears any resemblance whatsoever to the armed civilian militias that have evolved recently as part of the extremist antigovernment movement. These militias have no authority or protection to exist or organize under either the Constitution or federal law.

That was the short answer. The long answer involves a bit more historical analysis concerning the origins and evolution of the militias from the colonial period to 1903, when the National Guard was formally established by Congress.

During the colonial period armed volunteer citizens banded together as militias and took part in frontier battles against Native Americans and the French. During the years leading up to the Revolutionary War, these militias served as the armed forces of the various states, as the de facto army of the prerevolutionary nation, and fought against the British troops in the earliest skirmishes of the Revolutionary War. The Minutemen of Massachusetts was one of these militias. This was the militia that encountered the British in Lexington and Concord and fired the "shot heard round the world" that marked the beginning of the Revolutionary War.

Because these militias were neither organized nor reliable enough to defeat the British, the Continental Congress founded the Continental Army, a more effective fighting force. George Washington was appointed to command the Continental Army, which ultimately succeeded in defeating the British troops. During the war, armed volunteer militias assisted the Continental Army, but it is generally recognized that these militias did not play a pivotal role in the colonists' victory.

Following the war, however, a lively debate ensued about the wisdom of maintaining a standing federal army, and whether this army constituted a threat to the territorial security and political sovereignty of the individual states, to the extent that such limited sovereignty would exist within the context of the new union.

The Federalists, who supported a strong federal government, also supported the maintenance of a strong federal army. The

Anti-Federalists, who feared a strong central government and a standing federal army, argued that the Continental Army should be disbanded and replaced by the traditional force of state militias.

This was a debate of considerable weight and importance at the time, and ultimately resulted in the constitutional provisions for "well-regulated state militias"—the Militia Clauses of the Constitution and the Second Amendment to the Bill of Rights—and in a system of shared state and federal control over the militias. For example, the Militia Clauses give Congress authority to organize, arm, and discipline the state militias when in federally mandated service, while the states under the Militia Clauses retain power over the appointment of officers and the implementation of training.

Elsewhere in the Constitution, Article II establishes the president as commander in chief of the state militias when they are called into federal service.

I think it would be valuable to reproduce for the record the Militia Clauses and Article II of the Constitution to see what the Constitution actually says about the militias. The Militia Clauses read:

> The Congress shall have Power
> [15] To provide for calling forth the Militia to execute the Laws of the Union, suppress Insurrections and repel Invasion;
> [16] To provide for organizing, arming, and disciplining the Militia, and for governing such part of them as may be employed in the Service of the United States, reserving to the States respectively, the Appointment of the Officers, and the Authority of training the Militia according to the discipline prescribed by Congress.

And Article II reads in part:

> The President shall be Commander in Chief of the Army and Navy of the United States, and of the Militia of the several States, when called into the actual Service of the United States....

The state militia referenced in the Militia Clauses of the Constitution and in Article II, is regulated by the president, the Congress, and the governors of the states. It is in fact the very same state militia that is referred to in the Second Amendment as the "well-regulated militia" that possesses the right under the amendment to keep and bear arms.

Also, one should note the mission of the militia as described in the Militia Clauses: to execute the laws of the union and to suppress insurrections. Thus, the mission of the state militia established by the Constitution is very different from the mission of the armed civilian militias that are threatening acts of antigovernment violence, and in some cases actually committing these kinds of acts. The mission of the militia established by the Constitution is to repel and suppress insurrections against the government; the articulated mission of many of the armed civilian militias, whose existence is not sanctioned by the Constitution, is to foment insurrection against the government.

The militia referenced in the Constitution—a well-regulated military body with the president, the Congress, and the state governors sharing command, control, and regulatory authority—is quite a contrast to the armed civilian militias that have no legal connection whatsoever with either the Constitution, the president, the Congress, or the state governments. The state militias sanctioned by the Constitution are government-regulated bodies, and there is in fact a two-hundred-year history of government regulation of the state militias.

In 1792, acting upon its authority under the Militia Clauses, the Congress passed the Militia Act,[2] which established mandatory service in the state militias, as well as membership and duty requirements. However, throughout the 1800s, public support and participation in the militias waned, and mandatory militia service was phased out. By 1877, when state officials formed the National Guard Association, state militias became known as the National Guard. And, in 1903, the Congress passed the Dick Act which established the modern National Guard, replacing the state militias as they were defined in the federal act of 1792.

Let me just repeat something, because it is so important: Both the National Guard, as established by congressional legislation in 1903, and the unorganized militia, as established by the same piece of legislation, were established as government bodies to be utilized and regulated by governmental authorities—in some areas by the state governments, and in other areas by the federal government. This is an important point because the armed civilian militias that are organizing today are doing so outside of any constitutional or statutory authority, and in many cases are organizing and training in violation of state laws that prohibit private armies and paramilitary training. So for this reason and others, when these armed civilian militias claim that they possess constitutional authority to organize and train, it is important to recognize that they have no such authority.

Also, many of the civilian militias are not only organizing and operating outside of the authority of the established federal and state governments—the constitutional legitimacy of which they reject—but in fact view themselves as acting on behalf of what they regard as the true legitimate government of the United States, as they define it. Obviously, for the rest of us, this is highly problematic because neither we nor the Constitution subscribes to their contorted view of our government. So it is worth emphasizing that these private militias are operating outside of governmental authority. In their very existence and nature they are totally contrary to the "well-regulated militia" established by the Constitution and federal law.

A.P. In what way do the militias view the current government as illegitimate? Do they view the current president and Congress as illegitimate, or do they condemn the entire system of federal government as established by the Constitution?

B.L. They view the entire system of federal government as having evolved out of control. They do not view the Clinton administration or the current Congress as illegitimate per se, but they might see the Clinton administration and the Congress as symptomatic of the overall problem of government. So what comes under their indictment is the whole federal system—the Constitution as we know it, the three branches of the federal government, and federal regulatory and law enforcement agencies.

The militias have a rather substantial laundry list of grievances against the government which, in their minds, reflects the tyrannical nature of the federal government. As a result they feel that they have not only the option but the duty to implement their own government, which they see as the true government intended by the founders of this country. This is nonsense, but it is nevertheless what many in this movement believe.

A.P. What is the laundry list of grievances? Many of us have complaints about the government, but what is the nature of the grievances in this case that is so severe that it supposedly justifies dissolving the constitutional framework of the federal government? Is the charge that the federal government is encroaching on civil liberties, or does this have more to do with opposition to government regulations?

B.L. Both of these areas are implicated by the militias. There is a perception that the government, through too much regulation, is violating people's civil liberties and generally interfering too much in people's lives.

If you look at the social surveys, an area of concern among Americans today is the role of the federal government in the lives of individual citizens. That was one of the core issues that determined the last election in 1994, and it will probably play an important role in the election in 1996. For the purposes of our discussion here, this concern is grounded in several distinct areas: (a) land management and environmental regulations that in some parts of the country impact on traditional livelihoods such as ranching, farming, mining, and logging; (b) government restrictions on the purchase and possession of firearms; (c) taxes; and (d) social issues, such as abortion, gay rights, and public schools.

Over the last half century or so, basically since the New Deal, the federal government has enacted a myriad of regulations relating to industry, commerce, land use, and the environment. Many of these regulations are necessary and beneficial, and, arguably, many perhaps are burdensome. The ideal government regulation theoretically strikes a perfect balance between protecting public and private interests. But there is probably no such thing as a government regulation that perfectly strikes this balance. So on the one hand, we regard clean air and clean water favorably. Gun-control laws are in place in every civilized country to help protect public safety. However, to the extent that government regulations seeking to protect public safety and the environment interfere with people's individual lives, these regulations often become the object of a great deal of anger and frustration.

This dichotomy between public and private interests exists with respect to most government regulations. Perhaps the government could do a better job of addressing the concerns of the private interests impacted by government regulations. But there is no credible argument that can be made that regulations duly enacted by the federal government are unconstitutional. And this is precisely the claim of many antigovernment extremists, including many of the armed civilian militias.

A.P. What is your sense of the role that racism plays in militia ideology and in the militia movement? In the previous chapter, Thomas Halpern characterized the militia movement as being primarily an antigovernment rebellion, with racism and anti-Semitism playing a supporting role, but not a dominant one.

B.L. I think that is probably accurate, though white supremacy arguably fuels the engine of this movement, and its role should not be underestimated. Ever since the government of this country began rejecting invidious racial discrimination, there has been a tension between those who believe in discrimination and those who do not. Going back to my brief remarks about federal regulation, most African Americans view the federal government and federal regulation as primary mechanisms for protecting their civil rights and civil liberties, while many white Americans increasingly view the federal government as an impediment to the fulfillment of their civil rights and civil liberties. So, to a certain extent, the racist movement in this country is, by definition, going to be antigovernment, because the primary means of eradicating racial discrimination is through public policy, legislation, and court cases.

So, to the extent that the government plays a role in eradicating a way of life that supporters of segregation hold dear, racist and antigovernment attitudes will often coexist comfortably. In other words, racists will be antigovernment, but the opposite will not always be true; there are many people with extreme antigovernment views who are not racists. But there is a synergistic relationship developing here, because racists are establishing bridges to a broad spectrum of people who are against the government, not because they are racists, but because they do not like taxes, or what is being taught in the public schools, or what is going on with abortion rights or gun control.

However, to the extent that there is an engine driving the militia movement, in terms of the leadership, there is a clear and unambiguous racist connection to much of the leadership of the movement. And the racist leadership is saying, "Look, we are antigovernment too, we all can agree on a core set of principles: that the government is destroying our way of life and is the biggest threat to us." So, if that is your core belief—that the government is your enemy—your basis for opposing the government becomes less important, and this allows for the establishment of relationships among groups with various agendas that might not have been possible only a few years ago.

Waco and Ruby Ridge and the passage of the Brady bill were events that most people in the antigovernment movement, racist and nonracist alike, related to as evidence that ratified their worst fears about government. The significance of these events was that they transformed the antigovernment movement into an umbrella movement that now more or less accommodates disparate groups that were not previously aligned or united. Up to this point, tax protesters did not necessarily care about regulations for clean water, and home schooling supporters did not necessarily care about environmental restrictions on logging. There is a saying, "the enemy of my enemy is my friend," which I think is appropriately applied here. But I also think that racists who have a history of antigovernment ideology, and who also have a predisposition to-ward paramilitarism, are making a concerted effort to aligning themselves with the militia component of the antigovernment movement, which is a natural fit for them anyway.

By operating with a stealth bigotry, racist groups can open up many more avenues to recruit potential members. If you walk down the street with a robe and a hood, you would probably turn off a lot of people. But if you talk in coded terms of antigovernment rhetoric, which to some extent many mainstream Americans can relate to, you are likely to appeal to more people and attract more members.

A.P. Let me make one more distinction, this time between militias and antigovernment extremists. A member of an armed civilian militia is likely to be an antigovernment extremist, but an antigovernment extremist is not necessarily a member of a militia group. In other words, would you say that the antigovernment movement is the broader overarching movement, and that the militias are the paramilitary wing of the movement?

B.L. Yes, I think that is accurate. But I want to be clear about the fact that we are talking about a very amorphous movement. We are not talking about a professional association. There is no official structure or membership to the antigovernment movement.

As to the militias, there are some groups which call themselves militias that are not militias at all in the sense of acting as the para-military wing of the antigovernment movement, while others that call themselves information groups or hunting clubs do in fact constitute such militias. The best way to identify the components of the militia movement is to look not at a group's label, but at its characteristics.

A.P. I want to discuss the connection between the antigovern-ment extremists as Constitutionalists and Patriots and the racist influence. What, if anything, do the Constitutionalists contrib-ute to the synergy between the antigovernment and racist senti-ments? For example, the Constitutionalists only recognize the legitimacy of the first ten amendments to the Constitution—the

Bill of Rights—that were enacted in 1791, but they do not recognize the legitimacy of the amendments enacted thereafter.

B.L. Those militia members who call themselves Constitutionalists recognize only part of the Constitution, yet they totally misconstrue even the part that they purport to recognize. In their perverted analysis, blacks are not citizens and women cannot vote because Constitutionalists do not recognize the legitimacy of modern constitutional amendments. They refuse to accept that the Constitution itself is a fluid document in the sense that it allows for its own evolution through the enactment of amendments. That is central to the Constitution, and these Constitutionalists reject that.

They reject out of hand other important substantive components of the Constitution, such as the Supremacy and Property Clauses, because they interfere with their assertion of county supremacy over federal lands. Their readings of state power and federal authority in the Ninth and Tenth Amendments are just totally wrong. I do not want to give them even one iota of legitimacy in the way that they interpret the Constitution.

Having said all of that, let me answer your question about the synergy between the racist influences and this view of the Constitution. The Christian Identity movement, which has ties to the current leadership of the militia movement, is a movement that regards the United States as the New Jerusalem, regards whites as being the inheritors of this New Jerusalem, and regards blacks and Jews as subhuman and evil, and not worthy to live with whites.

Now I have to be clear about something. Christian Identity, notwithstanding its name, is a thorough rejection of what we know as Christianity. It is, at its core, a white supremacist religion that rejects the teachings of Christ himself. So I do not want there to be any ambiguity about the nature of this movement. It is not a Christian movement in the sense that we know Christianity theologically.

The Christian Identity movement can coexist very comfortably with the Constitutionalists in the antigovernment movement because, ideologically, they are very compatible. For example, the

Constitutionalists do not recognize the Thirteenth Amendment to the Constitution, which abolished slavery. Not recognizing the abolition of slavery in the United States is compatible with the characterization in Christian Identity of African Americans as subhuman. So although the philosophical and ideological orientation may not be precisely aligned between the white supremacists and the Constitutionalists, the end result is often virtually the same. If you do not recognize the abolition of slavery as the law of the land in the United States, then chances are you are not going to have a problem with the Christian Identity assertion that African Americans are subhuman.

A.P. What is the relationship between the leaders of Christian Identity and the leaders of the militia movement? For example, there was a famous meeting in Estes Park, Colorado in 1992, which was convened by Christian Identity Pastor Pete Peters, and attended by Klansmen, neo-Nazis, tax protesters, home schoolers, extreme gun rights activists, and future militia leaders. Speakers at the conference included Louis Beam, a former head of the Ku Klux Klan in Texas, and Larry Pratt, head of the Gun Owners of America and currently on leave as co-chair of Patrick Buchanan's presidential campaign.

B.L. The meeting at Estes Park was called shortly after the confrontation had ended between Randy Weaver and federal authorities at Ruby Ridge. At this meeting, previously disparate and unconnected groups came together and became the early organizers and members of the extremist antigovernment movement that we see today, of which the militia movement is a part. As I said before, "the enemy of my enemy is my friend," and this was the general bonding ethic of the group—the enemy in this case being the federal government.

A.P. What role did the Randy Weaver incident at Ruby Ridge play in motivating people to have this meeting?

B.L. For the attendees at Estes Park, Randy Weaver symbolized the Everyman who is victimized by a tyrannical government. In fact, Weaver is a self-described white separatist linked to the Christian Identity movement, and had been charged with trafficking in firearms in violation of federal law. When Weaver defied a federal order to appear in court, federal authorities surrounded his home in northern Idaho, and this essentially became the stand-off at Ruby Ridge, which ultimately resulted in three fatalities: Randy Weaver's wife and son as well as a dedicated federal agent. From the perspective of the antigovernment extremists, Randy Weaver is a victim of the government tyranny they fear—a validation of their extremist beliefs.

Actually, I should note that Weaver was not charged with a very significant violation of firearms laws. I believe the charges involved only one or two sawed-off shotguns, and he was eventually acquitted of those charges, though he was convicted for his initial failure to appear in federal court. Also, congressional hearings were held on the Weaver incident, five high-ranking FBI officials were demoted, and the FBI's policy regarding the use of force was reexamined. The behavior of some of the federal agents involved in this incident appears to have been improper with regard to the resort to deadly force. But the extremists have extrapolated from the tragic mistakes that took place at Ruby Ridge, and have applied them across the board to every federal law enforcement agent, arguing that the entire federal government is a tyranny that requires an armed citizen response on a mass scale.

A.P. One of the things that Thomas Halpern and I talked about in the preceding section is the paradoxical claim of the militias that they are oppressed by a tyrannical government, when in fact our country probably allows more civil liberties than any other country. For example, the current free speech standards in the United States are more permissive than in virtually any other country. The United States is the only industrialized country that does not have comprehensive gun-control laws. And we have perhaps the lowest tax rates of any industrial country.

B.L. Your point is well taken, but we need to look at the context in which these people view this issue.

Our country was founded by rugged individualists who became accustomed to making decisions in their lives relatively unconstrained by governmental regulation. This era, when people moved west to settle the country with their guns and families, is romanticized by the antigovernment movement as a utopian period in the country's history. A man could build his own house, farm and ranch almost totally free of any kind of government regulation.

But that era is long past; there were far fewer people in the country then, our natural resources were abundant and pristine, and there were no modern communication or transportation systems, which made whatever government regulations that might have existed less enforceable.

Today we are a country of over 260 million people, resources are scarcer, and there is a heightened concern for protecting the environment. In addition, we also have highly developed communication and transportation systems that make previously secluded areas of the country accessible to almost anyone. As a result, the need for government regulation of even remote public resources has become apparent, and the government now has the ability to monitor compliance and enforce these laws.

Now, many of these grievances about the federal government being tyrannical have to do with the clash between the desire of private interests to commercially develop public resources on federal land, and the desire to preserve these resources for environmental reasons. But many of these individuals' concerns about the federal government being tyrannical also stem from their refusal to recognize the government's interest in managing public resources.

In general, a debate about the reach of federal authority is certainly appropriate if it takes place within an informed and balanced view of federal power and its constitutional parameters. But what we have seen recently, even within one of our mainstream political parties, is the emergence of a radical advocacy of a decentralized and demobilized federal government, as well as the emergence of this extreme antigovernment movement that has connections with white supremacists and armed militias.

The idea of a federal government turned tyrannical is also disseminated by fringe Second Amendment extremists and gun-rights activists who have charged that the passage of recent gun-control laws—the Brady bill and the assault weapons ban—demonstrate the government's inclination to violate the constitutional rights of citizens. There is also a notion among extremists that federal gun-control laws are part of a United Nations or New World Order plot to disarm American citizens.

With regard to the claim that the federal government is conspiring with the United Nations and the New World Order to take over the country, I am not even going to dignify this charge with a response. It is completely ludicrous. As to the charge that gun control violates the Second Amendment rights of American citizens, this comes out of the misguided idea that the Second Amendment gives private individuals the right to keep and bear arms. This is an important issue that I would like to address in more detail later in the interview. For now I would point out that the rights granted under the Second Amendment do not apply to individual citizens, but to the "well-regulated militia" referenced in the amendment.

In response to your question about why so many people feel threatened by the government even though as individuals we probably have more freedom here than in any other country, it depends on how people define these rights. Those in the antigovernment movement have expanded their notion of individual rights beyond that which the Constitution actually provides, and have fallen into a conspiracy mentality that is irrational and, again, has little to do with what the Constitution and constitutional rights are about.

In short, much of this talk about federal tyranny has to do with people claiming rights which simply do not exist. If you are someone who believes that whites are superior and blacks are inferior, the fact that an antidiscrimination law or a hate-crime law exists is going to be a big problem for you. And if you are someone who believes that the government has no right to tax a portion of your income, the fact that there are taxes is going to shake you to the core. Likewise, if you believe that you have a constitutional right to possess and purchase any kind of firearm at any time with no restrictions, then you will view gun control as evidence of a tyrannical government. Or if you claim a sovereign right as an individual citizen to use federal land in any way that you wish, then you will view federal land management and environmental regulations as tyrannical.

The fact is that the federal government has the constitutional authority to do all of these things—to enact antidiscrimination and gun-control laws, to tax people's income, and to regulate federal lands. But the notion that the government does not have this authority makes many people see the government as the biggest enemy and threat to their way of life.

A.P. Does this notion of Americans as rugged individualists help explain the geographical concentration of the antigovernment movement in the West and other rural regions?

B.L. I think that there is a connection to some extent, although this is a very complex movement. The people who are against land-use and environmental regulations are much more likely to be in rural areas, or in western states where much of the land is owned by the federal government. And you also have Second Amendment extremists who are active in this movement, who generally also live in rural areas, including the West. The same is true for tax protesters. So, yes, if you want to describe the movement generally, it is not a metropolitan movement. If you look at the proponents of this movement—tax protesters, land-use protesters, home-schooling proponents, Second Amendment extremists—the kinds of concerns they have are less prominent in urban areas.

Can I interject one more thing about this? Many people in this movement look at urban America as an example of what the future is for them in their regions unless some things change. And for them this is a bleak future. It is a future of racial integration, crime, and bloated government bureaucracies that fail to take care of people who are trying to do what's best for their families. This is a complex and complicated picture, which merits a focused discussion of its own. But this picture of a deteriorated urban America is another reason why this movement is largely rural, and not centered in metropolitan areas of the country.

A.P. It seems that many of the political grievances that people in this movement have cannot ever be remedied to their satisfaction, if, in fact, they see antidiscrimination laws, gun-control laws, and environmental laws as unconstitutional. But what about the economic grievances, which are implicit in the movement's opposition to federal regulations to the extent that they impact on jobs? Does this movement have legitimate economic grievances that might be remedied by increased government sensitivity to the impact of environmental laws and land-use regulations on jobs? I am not saying by any means that the environment should not be a government priority. But does the socioeconomic context of the movement, if there is one, shed any light on its sociopolitical framework?

B.L. Well, the sociopolitical aspects of the movement are very telling. There is a nationwide discussion taking place today regarding the appropriate role of the federal government. That is a legitimate topic for political debate. And if you look at the social surveys, close to one in four Americans believes that democracy does not work for them anymore; one in three is angry about what is taking place in society; and half the population does not think the legal system works for them anymore. So there is a large body of people out there who think that the government does not work well for them on a number of levels.

But there is a big difference between saying that something is not working well and needs to be fixed through legal and political mechanisms, and contending as the extremists do that the government is illegitimate and declaring outright war against it.

If you talk to most American citizens, they will have a different suggestion as to how the government can do better. But most people will say that the appropriate response is to work through existing peaceful mechanisms, through the political process, through education, through the press, through a variety of legal means that have made our Constitution the oldest Constitution in the world, and one that is and has been a model for many other countries.

But what we have with the antigovernment extremists is this badly distorted notion of the Constitution that rejects the very basis of our government, and rejects many of the goals and aspirations of mainstream Americans. Anyone can say there is something wrong. But the question is, does that mean we destroy democracy and the Constitution to deal with the problem? Those in the antigovernment movement say yes.

But the Declaration of Independence, which many antigovernment extremists look to as some kind of rallying cry, itself says that "[p]rudence, indeed, will dictate that Governments long established should not be changed for light and transient causes; and accordingly all experience hath shewn, that mankind are more disposed to suffer, while evils are sufferable, than to right themselves by abolishing the forms to which they are accustomed." This basically means that we should approach problems head-on without destroying democracy. Democracy did not create these problems.

Our founders put together a system that can be confounding. If you want to solve problems in an immediate and unambiguous fashion, hire a dictator. Our process, with its checks and balances, in many ways is supposed to be a maze. It is supposed to put up obstacles against certain kinds of fundamental change; the reason being that if we have these checks and balances, and if we have a marketplace of ideas, we might not get an immediate solution, but we are likely to get a well-thought-out solution, and we are likely to get one that reflects the democratic ideals upon which our country is founded.

For many people, this is frustrating. But it is important to recognize that, in a democracy such as ours, although we often do not like the result we get, the process itself is a legitimate one. And that is a fundamentally important concept to note.

A.P. That was well stated, and is more important than the point I asked you about. And I would like to get to some of the specific constitutional questions involved in a moment or so. But the concern expressed in my previous question was an economic question. And although a reasonable person would not recognize the validity of the constitutional claims of this extremist movement, a reasonable person might recognize the legitimacy of the economic grievances of the movement, to the extent that they are voiced.

We used to have solid family farms and good manufacturing jobs in our factories. Loggers and ranchers used to have secure futures. Constitutional questions aside, it does not seem to be good policy for the government to ignore the struggle to make a living that is taking place in some areas.

B.L. I think that your main point is a valid one. People's expectations about their security and their future have changed over the last twenty years. The skills that are needed today to be employed are different than what was needed before. The security that used to exist in the agrarian and manufacturing sectors is not there today. The family farm is a threatened institution. I wish this were not the case. And there might be policies available to the government that would respond better to this shift in our economy, and the decline in manufacturing and family farming. But it might be that the shift and decline are a function of changes that lie largely outside of governmental influence.

Whatever the case may be, we are experiencing some breathtaking changes in our country. There are many possible responses to these changes that can be pursued within the framework of our constitutional system, and I certainly hope that people will become involved in protecting their farms and their jobs to the extent that they are capable—but, again, within the existing framework of the law, and within the existing framework of legitimate government oversight.

A.P. We mentioned earlier that the militia movement is more or less the paramilitary arm of the extremist antigovernment movement. How much of a threat to civil order are the militias, and how much of a threat do these private armies pose to democratic institutions?

B.L. I think there are two levels of threat here. On one level, simply having a militia around is intimidating, even if they ultimately do nothing. It is very unsettling to have this proliferation of armed bodies of organized private individuals ready for armed conflict. And to the extent that private individuals are engaged in paramilitary training and military organizing, that is something that can and should be regulated because of the threat it poses.

Our society is based on addressing and resolving societal problems through various peaceful mechanisms. This might not be the most efficient way to do business, but it is most likely to result in a peaceful resolution of grievances that reflects the view of a majority of our citizens, while at the same time protecting the rights of the minority. So on this level, the threat that exists is the threat of intimidation, simply by virtue of the fact that some private citizens are militarily organized, heavily armed, and extensively trained for violence against the peaceful conduct of government and public business.

On another level, militia members and armed extremists are actually threatening governmental officials and interfering with their ability to do their jobs properly. We have a range of government employees, including judges, prosecutors, tax collectors, forest rangers, and police, who are actually being threatened or met with violence from antigovernment extremists. And this has happened and is happening in many parts of the country.

There was an incident in Fowlerville, Michigan, where some militia members were arrested with sophisticated weapons and surveillance equipment, and there were notes found suggesting that they had law enforcement agents under surveillance. In Montana a judge has been performing her duties under death threats for many months now. In central California a county official was stabbed by antigovernment extremists. Just very recently in the state of Texas, antigovernment extremists declared that the government of the state of Texas was illegitimate, and that they were setting up their own government. There also have been incidents where antigovernment extremists have actually taken over courtrooms. In other incidents, these extremists have threatened to kidnap government officials and prosecutors who refused to dismiss traffic violations against them. And this is merely a short summary of what is happening. We could fill several pages of this book with all of the incidents such as these that have taken place. So the actual threat and use of violence against public officials by antigovernment extremists is a pretty widespread phenomenon at this point.

A.P. You were just describing the conduct of armed antigovernment extremists. Does this mean that militia members are not the only members of the antigovernment movement who are armed with firearms or weapons?

B.L. In terms of definitions, a militia refers to a body of armed persons who are organized and trained for armed conflict and follow a command structure. Some of those in the antigovernment movement who commit or threaten acts of violence are not technically members of a militia. They may be acting in a small group that really does not fit the technical definition of a military body, but still they are armed and threaten people. A lone political assassin might not be a member of a militia, but still is a serious threat to public officials and civil order.

A.P. What you described a moment ago was the commission of crimes by antigovernment extremists. Many of these crimes are preceded by speech threatening criminal activity. What is the legal status of speech that threatens these kinds of crimes?

B.L. Are you talking about the extremists who are actually committing these offenses, or other extremists?

A.P. I am talking about extremists who are actually committing the offenses, and also extremists who have not committed these kinds of offenses, but who pose a credible threat to committing these kinds of offenses.

B.L. I see what you are getting at, and I think that much would depend on what you mean by "credible threat." But certainly there is a significant amount of rhetoric that often accompanies these incidents. These incidents involve people who are carrying out their terrorist political objectives. Intimidating public officials or obstructing them in the administration of their duties is a crime, as are the traditional crimes of assault and making threats.

Now, to the extent that there is another category of people who crank up those in the movement to commit these crimes, there is not much that you can do from a legal standpoint. If I say that the government is tyrannical and illegitimate and that government officials should be dealt with accordingly, or broadly and amorphously advocate violence in the abstract, that is protected speech.

A.P. What constitutes intimidation of a public official such that it becomes a crime? Can the crime of intimidation of a public official be either a threat or an act of violence?

B.L. Certainly. If you look at the Montana penal code, for example, section 45-7-102, the title reads, "Threats and other improper influences of an official in political matters." A person commits an offense under this section if he "purposely or knowingly threatens harm to a public official or their family members to influence a decision, opinion, recommendation, or a vote," or basically in the exercise of their official duties. There are other similar statutes in other states as well. So, yes, any kind of threat directed at a public official that is designed to intimidate him or her in the exercise of their official duties is a crime.

A.P. So if a number of extremists have organized in their locality and threaten retaliation against a judge if a ruling goes against their wishes, is that a crime?

B.L. Most probably. But what you are asking me is more a question of fact than of law. If it can be shown that the threat is a bona fide threat, then the threat can be punished. Remember as well that it is a crime to interfere with judicial proceedings.

A.P. So the mere issuance of a threat against a public official is not necessarily a crime. In order for a threat to be a crime, the threat has to be credible; there has to be some plausibility that the threat actually will be carried out.

B.L. That's right. There was a case called *Watts v. United States,*[3] where an African American who had just been drafted said, "If I am drafted the first person that I am going to get in my gun sights is LBJ," referring to President Lyndon Johnson. And the courts ruled that although the statute is indeed a valid statute and punishes threats against the president, the threat in this case was really a crude political statement made at the height of the Vietnam War, and not a bona fide threat to shoot the president.

So whether a threat issued against a public official constitutes a crime depends on the context in which the threat is issued. Whether you have the ability to carry out the threat, whether the threat is directed at a particular person, or whether the threat specifies an attack at a particular time—these are the kinds of things that determine the criminality of a threat against a public official.

A.P. What if a threat has a relatively low chance of actually being carried out, but it is intimidating enough to influence the behavior of a judge or a legislator? To receive a threat of violence is very disturbing. And it may be that the mere fact of the threat, however implausible, is enough to influence the behavior of a judge or legislator in many instances. It might give one cause to say, Why take a chance and not do what this person wants me to do? And it may be that the intent of the threat was not to carry out the threat, but to intimidate the public official into changing his or her behavior. It seems to me the issue of whether a threat is a crime or not would need to address not only the safety of public officials, but also protection of the integrity of the democratic and judicial processes.

B.L. Again, as the Montana statute says, if a person knowingly threatens harm to a person with the purpose of influencing a decision, that is a crime. Now, of course, you have to remember that we are talking about issues relating more to fact than to law, and what you have to do, if you are a prosecutor, is convince a jury that a crime took place.

A.P. Many leaders of the extremist antigovernment movement have issued threats directed at officials in Washington from places that are several hundred miles away. Let us assume, for the sake of argument, that there is a relatively small chance that these threats will ever be carried out. But that small chance is enough to intimidate a judge or legislator into changing behavior, making a particular judicial ruling, or casting a vote on legislation.

B.L. Again, the criminality or noncriminality of a threat depends on the factual context in which the threat is issued. Generally, there has to be an apparent ability to carry out the threat in order for it to be a crime. The mere advocacy of violence in the abstract is not a criminal offense. However, if there is an actual plan to commit a crime at some point in the future, then certainly this kind of speech can be punished as part of a conspiracy or criminal plan.

But what you are describing sounds more to me like the situation in the *Watts* case or in *Brandenburg v. Ohio*,[4] where the threats issued were held by the Supreme Court to not be punishable under the Constitution. However, once you cross the line and issue either what is regarded as a credible threat, or engage in a conspiracy, that is, when you plan to commit a crime, then certainly punishment is warranted.

Right now the test for this kind of speech, that is, the issuance of threats or use of incendiary speech, is the *Brandenburg* test. And this test requires that a couple of elements be satisfied. Let me give you some factual background to the case.

During the 1960s Clarence Brandenburg was at a Ku Klux Klan rally, which was filmed by a television news crew. And he said a variety of things that were generally hateful, that were anti-Semitic and anti-African American. Why don't I read for the record the unanimous opinion of the Court with regard to the facts, which have some relevance to your concerns about the constitutionality of threats directed at public officials. Here is how the Court described the facts:

> The record shows that a man, identified at trial as the appellant [that is, Clarence Brandenburg], telephoned an announcer-reporter on the staff of a Cincinnati television station and invited him to come to a Ku Klux Klan "rally" to be held at a farm in Hamilton County. With the cooperation of the organizers, the reporter and a cameraman attended the meeting and filmed the events. Portions of the films were later broadcast on the local station and on a national network.
>
> The prosecutor's case rested on the films and on testimony identifying the appellant as the person who spoke at the rally. The State also introduced into evidence several articles appearing in the film, including a pistol, a rifle, a shotgun, ammunition, a Bible, and a red hood worn by the speaker in the films.
>
> One film showed twelve hooded figures, some of whom carried firearms. They were gathered around a large wooden cross, which they burned. No one was present other than

the participants and the newsmen who made the film. Most of the words uttered during the scene were incomprehensible when the film was projected, but scattered phrases could be understood that were derogatory of Negroes and, in one instance, of Jews. Another scene on the same film showed the appellant in Klan regalia, making a speech. The speech, in full, was as follows:

> This is an organizers' meeting. We have had quite a few members here today which are—we have hundreds and hundreds of members throughout the state of Ohio. I can quote from a newspaper clipping from the Columbus, Ohio Dispatch, five weeks ago Sunday morning. The Klan has more members in the State of Ohio than does any other organization, but if our President, our Congress, our Supreme Court, continues to suppress the white, Caucasian race, it's possible that there might have to be some revengeance taken.
>
> We are marching on Congress July the Fourth, four hundred thousand strong. From there we are dividing into two groups, one group to march on St. Augustine, Florida, the other group to march into Mississippi. Thank you.[5]

In the *Brandenburg* case, the Supreme Court looked at an Ohio statute called the Ohio Criminal Syndicalism Statute. That statute prohibited the advocacy of a crime, or the advocacy of violence as a means of carrying out industrial or political reform. This Ohio statute prohibited "advocat[ing] ... the duty, necessity, or propriety of crime, sabotage, violence, or unlawful methods of terrorism as a means of accomplishing industrial or political reform [and for] voluntarily assembl[ing] with any society, group, or assemblage of persons formed to teach or advocate the doctrines of criminal syndicalism."

Now, in a unanimous *per curiam* opinion, the Supreme Court threw out that statute without even applying Brandenburg's speech. A *per curiam* opinion is simply a unanimous opinion, the authorship of which is not attributed to any particular justice. And they articulated what is now the modern test to determine what constitutes illegal incitement. Incitement is one of several areas of speech that is unprotected by the First Amendment, and thus is generally subject to government regulation.

This test requires two elements in order for dangerous advocacy to be considered incitement, and therefore unprotected speech: first, the speech must be directed to inciting or producing imminent lawless action; second, the speech must be likely to incite or produce such action. This was a significant evolution in free speech jurisprudence. Previously, and I think many civil libertarians will tell you this, there were abuses of individuals who expressed virulent and sometimes abstractly violent antigovernment speech and they were punished for it, or were punished for their associations.

The *Brandenburg* opinion, however, ruled that there has to be a likelihood that the incitement will produce an imminent unlawful act in order for the speech to be punished.

A.P. What are the principle elements needed to establish a criminal act?

B.L. In order to prove a crime, you have to show that the person had a culpable mindset. For most crimes this means that you had to have the purpose or knowledge to commit the crime, and that you had to commit some kind of overt act.

A.P. What kind of act?

B.L. Sometimes the act can be very small. For instance, in a conspiracy, merely agreeing to the conspiracy can fulfill the act requirement. But you cannot punish someone for having a bad thought. The bad thought has to be accompanied by some affirmative illegal act.

A.P. What if the thought is articulated?

B.L. Generally, bad thoughts are not punishable, and neither is their expression punishable, and I think that is good. We do not want to punish people for thinking evil thoughts, we want to punish them for carrying out evil deeds.

Sometimes the illegality of that deed depends on the mindset of the person carrying out that deed. Let me give you an example.

If I turn over documents to you that are damaging to the United States without the intent of rendering aid or comfort to the enemy, and you are in fact a spy for the enemy, I am not guilty of treason. But if I turn over damaging documents with the intent of rendering aid and comfort to the enemy, then that same act becomes treasonous.

By the same token, the law looks at what a person's intent is, and you would have a difficult time proving beyond a reasonable doubt, which is the standard you need for conviction under the criminal law, that the intent behind the activities of many of these antigovernment extremists is criminal. Many people in this movement—though I think this is disingenuous—argue that their paramilitary activities are defensive, saying that they are just keeping weapons and training to defend themselves from a tyrannical government. If those activities are not independently a crime, you might have a difficult time proving the intent necessary to find them guilty of treason or some other crime.

Now, to the extent that they have automatic weapons, which are illegal, or they threaten someone, or they conduct paramilitary training or military organizing in states which have statutes proscribing that, they can certainly be prosecuted.

A.P. If the *Brandenburg* standard says that we cannot punish people for evil speech, but only for evil deeds, then basically what we are saying is that we are not capable of protecting the public from the harms of evil speech. There is little recognition of a need to balance the speech rights of an individual who engages in evil speech against the interests of the government to maintain civil order and to ensure the integrity of its own democratic foundations.

The *Brandenburg* standard does not even fit well within the "marketplace of ideas" model of the First Amendment. When one vendor of ideas in the marketplace is backing advocacy with threats of violence, as the antigovernment extremists are doing, what recourse does this leave the other participants in the marketplace? Who will step up and speak against violence under the threat of violent reprisal for doing so?

The threat of violence corrupts the marketplace and it should not be permitted. If a company submits a competitive bid for a government or private contract and threatens violence if it is not chosen, this would be a crime, regardless of the credibility of the threat. So where is the appropriate role for the threat of violence in the marketplace, whether it is a marketplace for commerce or a marketplace for speech?

And when you say we cannot regulate speech merely because it is offensive, I am not talking about regulating all offensive speech. But I am talking about regulating one very narrow category of offensive speech—the threat of violence issued against individuals and the government. Unlike speech which is merely offensive, threats have a much greater potential of undermining a person's sense of security and well-being, and of infiltrating and subverting the deliberative judicial and legislative processes. So why should we protect it? Do you see my point?

B.L. Yes, and, unfortunately, I disagree with it. Justice Brandeis once said that the fitting remedy for evil counsel is good counsel. And he argued that the government should not be in the business of enforcing fear and silence because fear breeds repression and this in turn breeds hate, and hate menaces a stable government. And this reflects the idea that just because certain kinds of speech are potentially hazardous, this does not mean that such speech should be limited, curtailed, or eradicated. And I would argue that the place to look to address your concerns is not at limiting speech. The place to look is at limiting activities that are harmful.

And this theory on which our First Amendment jurisprudence is based, the marketplace of ideas, which is set up to be as free as possible from government censorship, is important because of the democratic ideals it tries to embody. One of the ideas is that, in a democracy, good people will reject bad ideas. Another involves the Supreme Court's concern that it is far more dangerous for the government to establish an orthodoxy of acceptable ideas. This concern is reflected in some of the important First Amendment decisions by the Supreme Court, such as *Texas v. Johnson*,[6] the flag-burning case that was decided in 1989, and the *Watts* case that I mentioned.

Speech can repulse, it can upset, and it can even have the effect, unfortunately, of having some people react violently to it. But regarding the relationship between speech and violence, the Court has said that there must be a direct connection and imminency of violence, because otherwise one could argue that the Beatles' song "Helter Skelter" caused the Manson murders. And if the Supreme Court were ever to accept such an argument, where would we go from there? Wherever it would be, as a democracy that values free speech, we would not want to go there.

One of the things that is very important to grasp about this debate is the importance of protecting repulsive ideas. What is considered a repulsive idea today might be an acceptable idea tomorrow. Let me give you some brief examples. Much of what the abolitionists advocated before the Civil War was regarded by mainstream segments of the country as repulsive. The same thing could be said about the anti-war demonstrators during the Vietnam War. The grievances and marches of the civil rights movement were seen as repulsive in some communities. We want to be very careful to avoid limiting speech because we find it offensive or repulsive, even if there might be a potential hazard from that speech.

A.P. Under your standard, protection extends to harmful speech, even to speech that undermines our democratic institutions, as well as speech that arguably amounts to acts of terrorism directed at public and private individuals. This is what we are dealing with in terms of some of the speech engaged in by antigovernment extremists.

You mentioned Justice Brandeis as a source for the Court's First Amendment jurisprudence. His concurring opinion in *Whitney v. California*,[7] a Supreme Court case from the 1920s, is one of the most eloquent judicial statements on the First Amendment that we have. And his argument in that opinion certainly supports what you have been saying. But there was another Supreme Court justice who followed Justice Brandeis, Felix Frankfurter, who was concerned with the standard that was evolving in the Court's interpretation of the First Amendment. And Justice Frankfurter argued that a balancing of interests between harm and permissiveness ought to play a role in free speech law.

Recently, First Amendment scholars have criticized the *Brandenburg* standard as applied to incendiary speech because it protects speech that causes very significant harm to the democratic process, because it intimidates people from performing their federally mandated jobs, and threatens people's lives. For example, the militias are claiming that the recent passage of gun-control laws—the Brady bill and the assault weapons ban—is treasonous because in their minds it violates the Second Amendment. These militias have threatened duly-elected officials with execution for passing these laws, and have warned that if additional gun-control laws are passed, the legislators who vote for those laws will be executed. These threats are coming from people who are armed, who organize as private armies, and who conduct paramilitary training for violent action against the government. How can democracy be expected to function under these conditions?

If in fact these threats are changing the behavior of legislators, would it not be appropriate for judges to weigh the value of protecting those threats under the First Amendment with the harm those threats are causing to our democracy?

B.L. I think that you are playing both sides of the fence here. If these people are making a credible threat with the purpose of interfering with the duties of government officials, that can be punished.

A.P. But I am talking about threats that are not necessarily credible, but are damaging nevertheless. In addition to possibly intimidating judges and legislators, threats from armed militia groups also stifle the free speech of citizens in communities, who, absent the threat of militia violence, might speak out in public forums against the militias but do not for fear of violent retribution. This is terrorism. Kenneth Toole, director of the Montana Human Rights Network, writes:

Militia members are politically active, threatening public officials, talking about the need to "war" with their enemies. How comfortable would you be signing a letter to the editor, showing up at a community meeting, running for office?

The main impact of the militia movement has been its thuggish intimidation of grass-roots democracy in small communities across America. In some counties the fear created by the militia is akin to that produced in the South by the Ku Klux Klan in the 1960s. Public officials and private citizens actually have to weigh whether speaking their minds will result in an armed response from the local private armies.... This is serious business indeed and constitutes plain and simple terrorism.[8]

So although the threats issued by militias may not reflect imminent violence in many situations—though in some situations they might—they certainly do create a threat cloud that is infiltrating and poisoning our democratic institutions. So it seems that the *Brandenburg* standard does not apply in the absence of imminent violence, even where palpable harm occurs.

B.L. The standard does apply. The standard admits that there certainly are costs to free speech. Interestingly, the balancing approach for speech exists in Canada. But I think that the way the United States deals with it is the best way.

But let me address your remarks. Again, as I mentioned before, you are trying to have it both ways with the fact situation you are describing. If the threat is a credible one, and is issued with the requisite intent, and if a reasonable legislator or person would feel threatened, and if that could be proved in court, then the person making the threat could be punished. But the political history of this country has involved some offensive and radical expressions. Burning a public official in effigy is a very intimidating thing. Burning the American flag is an act that most Americans find very unpleasant. But the fact is that we as a society find that there is greater overall value in the expression of more speech than there is in the limitation of speech by government. And I think that you will be setting up a very dangerous precedent when you establish the government as the arbiter of what is acceptable speech. I am far more afraid of a government official in this regard, who has much greater ability to limit speech, than some kook out in the woods somewhere.

A.P. But even under current First Amendment jurisprudence, the government regulates a lot of speech.

B.L. But not based on the content.

A.P. Well, you could design a content-neutral restriction on threats of violence directed at the government as long as the restriction applied to right-wing threats as well as left-wing threats, or to threats motivated by whatever ideology.

B.L. That's true. But, again, if it's a threat it's a threat, and if it's not a threat, then it's not a threat. If we are talking about a continuum between pleasant political expression and downright criminal threat, there has to be room left for that very offensive, repulsive, repugnant, and even potentially hazardous speech.

A.P. Let me ask you another kind of question. What is the value to democratic discourse of the kinds of speech we are talking about, which antigovernment extremists engage in on a pretty regular basis? What is the value to a deliberative democracy of threats to assassinate public officials, such as the president and the attorney general, threats to overthrow the government by force, and hate speech directed at racial and ethnic groups? Does the First Amendment protect this degree of hate and violence? Distinguished constitutional law scholars, such as Cass Sunstein and Robert Bork, doubt whether the First Amendment protects this kind of speech.

B.L. And equally prominent constitutional law scholars, such as Professors Laurence Tribe and Gerald Gunther, argue differently.

If I may, I think there is an antidemocratic undergirding to your argument. In a democracy we want the free exchange of ideas. And with this free exchange we have an underlying trust that people will respond to good ideas and will reject bad ones. And what we should do, therefore, is allow debate of all kinds. And there are going to be some really horrible, incorrect, and really dumb ideas, but the place to ferret out these ideas is in the marketplace of ideas where people can see the facts laid straight out, and either accept or reject them.

A.P. Should the marketplace of ideas for speech be an absolutist libertarian market, or should there be some room for narrowly-targeted regulations of harmful speech? I do not think that we really want a totally *laissez-faire* market for either commerce or speech.

B.L. Show me a standard that you would put in place that does not have the potential to be abused. We have seen throughout our history, during World War I, during the Red Scare, and even right after the Revolutionary War, that there have been instances where the standards that you advocate have been consistently abused by government officials. They obviously did not share your concerns about balance and fairness and the integrity of the democratic process. An important thing to remember is that you would not be the person to administer your standard. People other than you in the government would be the caretakers of your standard, and these would be people perhaps with less integrity than you.

I really do fear the government more. Remember that the government has a tremendous degree of enforcement power that private citizens do not have. The government can put you in prison, it can take away your assets, and can launch investigations against you with the full weight of the state behind them. And that is a very different thing than having to deal with a kook who threatens you with violence, which, by the way, there are remedies for. If someone stalks me, if someone threatens me, if someone engages in paramilitary training with the intent to foment violence or civil disorder, then I have legal remedies to punish those acts.

And this is not to say that the government is the only possible means to prevent threats from escalating to the point where they endanger private persons or the government. An informed electorate, a watchdog press, and an informed community that rejects the kinds of speech you are concerned about could certainly deter or even put a stop to this. Let me give you an example. The Klan held a rally in Wyoming on Martin Luther King Day this year—and guess what?—practically everyone in Wyoming showed up to demonstrate against it. A similar thing happened in New Hampshire. Community norms can be a very effective deterrent to bad speech.

You can come up with so many scenarios where there is a potential hazard to speech or where there is a direct harm. I do not doubt for a second that there are many types of speech that result in harm. I think that Nazis parading through a community creates a palpable harm. But that is the cost of a free society.

A.P. I think it is possible to come up with a rigorous First Amendment standard that does balance, on the one side, the harm that the speech causes and, on the other side, the need to protect speech. We already do that kind of balancing within the current standards of interpretation. We have the strict scrutiny standard, which must be applied to restrictions on fundamental rights, and which requires a balancing between serving the government's compelling interests and the protection of fundamental rights. The government does have legitimate, compelling interests that it needs to protect. And under strict scrutiny, the restriction must be narrowly tailored and it must be effective to the extent that it accomplishes the government's compelling interest.

So the standard for fundamental rights already exists. But the *Brandenburg* standard does not permit this balancing to occur, or skews the balancing test so far in favor of permissive speech as to make the possibility for balancing nearly impossible. Militia members who are armed, who have formed private armies, who train for violence against the government, should not be permitted under the First Amendment to threaten the lives of government officials and private individuals. It is simply too dangerous and too harmful, and it deprives other people who do not practice violence of their legitimate rights.

B.L. I would agree with you in one way, and that is, to the extent that the government might restrict a certain kind of speech that does not involve content, certainly I would be more willing to accept regulation. That means, for instance, the proscription must apply equally to both the Boy Scouts and the Nazis. In other words, if the Boy Scouts are going to march on Main Street at 3 a.m., then I am going to enforce the law against them the same way that I would against the Nazis. What bothers me is that implicit in your argument is the tremendous potential to interfere with the communicative impact of speech, and that is something that modern First Amendment cases constrain the government from doing.

There are harms from speech. And, in fact, some of us might disproportionately bear the burdens of free speech. But the fact is that the Constitution constrains the government's interference with rights; the criminal law can address other types of interferences with rights.

One of the hallmarks of our First Amendment jurisprudence is the hesitation to implement prior restraint. Our society believes that it is far better to let the bad idea out and deal with the remedy later.

A.P. How do expressions of anti-Semitism and expressions of racial bigotry constitute political speech? Why do these kinds of speech not constitute racial libel?

B.L. Well, actually, that is interesting. The Supreme Court, in a case called *Beauharnais v. Illinois,*[9] dealt with an Illinois law that criminalized what was called group libel. And although that decision was never specifically overturned, it has basically been rejected by all of the modern First Amendment cases since.

But group libel happens to be a political expression. That someone might think that a certain group of persons is not worthy of societal rights is horrible, despicable, and antithetical to all of my religious and political beliefs. But nonetheless it is someone's idea of how he would structure society. And in that context I do not have a right to ban that speech. As much as I hate it and deplore it and would speak out against it, I would also vigorously support the right of some idiot to express those horrible views.

A.P. Would the *Brandenburg* standard extend to the speech of the militias to the point where they represented a plausible threat to overthrow the government, and where the verbalized threat of antigovernment violence became, I do not want to say imminent because that is the standard, but nudged up to the point of imminency? Does the *Brandenburg* standard protect speech to this degree?

B.L. The *Brandenburg* standard does. But if you have a criminal plan, such as a conspiracy to commit an illegal act, you do not need imminency. All you need is that criminal plan. So if people are actually planning to overthrow the government, and they are conspiring to do that, that can be punished. We have an adequate statutory framework to address the scenario that you just described. We can outlaw military organizing, we can outlaw paramilitary training, and we do outlaw criminal conspiracies, and we can even outlaw membership in groups if that membership meets certain criteria.

A.P. So what you are saying is that the remedy to the threat posed by the armed civilian militias does not lie within the realm of speech restriction, but that it lies within the realm of statutory law banning paramilitary training and the formation of private armies.

B.L. Absolutely. But I want to be sure to say that when speech becomes a bona fide criminal threat, it no longer has the protection that we normally give to expression. So in that case, speech loses its protection because it is a threat—threats are not protected.

I am talking about threat in the official, criminal, legal sense, not in the sense that you were conceptualizing it. A threat in the criminal, legal sense would be a direct threat with the apparent ability to carry it out against a recognizable target. Or, again, a conspiracy is another example where speech is unprotected. So there are plenty of instances where the spoken word can serve as the basis for a criminal prosecution.

A.P. So in your opinion, the remedy to the threat posed by armed civilian militias and antigovernment extremists who threaten violence is not to weaken the current First Amendment standard for incendiary speech, or to enact new categories of presumably prohibited speech, but to enforce existing state laws that ban private armies and paramilitary training, and to enact new federal statutes that do the same thing. And these measures are or would be constitutional.

B.L. That's correct. There are in fact plenty of available remedies to address the threat of violence posed by antigovernment extremists. Part of the problem that we have had in addressing this threat is that we have not fully utilized to date those laws and methods that we have at our disposal for dealing with extremist violence. For example, we can enact laws that ban paramilitary training; we can enact anti-militia laws which would ban private military organizing; we can pass laws that criminalize threats directed at government officials or that enhance the penalties attendant to those threats; we can criminalize impersonation of government officials, which would address those involved in these common law courts who impersonate judicial officers of the government; we can criminalize false instruments, such as counterfeit money orders and bogus liens that these people file with government officials to swindle or intimidate them; and we can also enforce existing weapons and explosives laws.

I think that the keys to addressing this issue are some of the tools that we already have at our disposal in various states. For example, seventeen states have laws on the books that ban paramilitary training, another seventeen states have laws that ban private armies, and another seven states have laws that ban both paramilitary training and private armies. Increased enforcement of these laws, though not always easy, is one of the available remedies that is constitutional. To the extent that there are states that do not have these laws, they should enact and enforce them.

There is also a federal statute that prohibits paramilitary training, but this law only punishes trainers; it does not punish the trainees. We should close this loophole to prohibit people from receiving paramilitary training and instruction.

At the Southern Poverty Law Center, we have proposed a model statute that closes this loophole. And we have proposed a model statute that prohibits the organization and maintenance of private armies.

These statutes, both at the state and federal level, are constitutional. My point is that there are remedies for this problem within the traditional criminal law context. We do not have to go out and create new areas of law or redefine our First Amendment protections as you have suggested.

A.P. You just mentioned that the anti-militia and anti-paramilitary training statutes are constitutional. The members of the armed militias would argue otherwise. They would argue that they have the right to possess firearms and train with these firearms under the Second Amendment, and that they have the right to assemble under the First Amendment.

B.L. I would be hard pressed to find any right for a group of private citizens to organize and maintain their own private army. That right simply does not exist. Nor do individuals have a right under the Second Amendment to possess firearms.

Perhaps the most misunderstood provision of our Constitution is the Second Amendment. The Second Amendment simply does not provide a private individual with the right to own or possess a firearm. Every modern federal court decision on the subject confirms this. Moreover, the Second Amendment does not give private citizens the right to establish and maintain their own private armies. The Second Amendment's "right to bear arms" has been interpreted by the courts to protect state-sponsored militias from undue federal interference.

Case law on the subject includes two Supreme Court cases—*United States v. Miller,*[10] and *Lewis v. United States.*[11]

The *Miller* case is the principal modern case on the Second Amendment. Here the Supreme Court formulated a Second Amendment rationale that is still used today. The case involved a violation of the 1934 National Firearms Act[12] by two defendants, who were charged with transporting an unregistered sawed-off shotgun in interstate commerce. The interstate commerce connection is important because that creates the basis for federal authority.

In *Miller,* the Court decided that the Second Amendment exists to protect state militias, and it is only in the context of the protection of state militias that the amendment should be analyzed and applied.

Basically the Court concentrated on whether or not the transportation or possession of an illegal sawed-off shotgun had any relation to the protection of a state militia. The Court analyzed the right found in the Second Amendment in relation to the preservation of a state militia, and simply found that individualized ownership of a sawed-off shotgun did not come within that right.

The *Lewis* case dealt with a provision in the 1968 Gun Control Act,[13] which prohibited the possession of guns by convicted felons. The Court looked at the hierarchy of constitutional rights, and looked at gun rights in the context of this hierarchy. Here, when I mention gun rights, I am referring to the right as it applies to the state militias, and not to individuals because the Second Amendment confers no individual right. In the *Lewis* case, the Court found that the right protected by the Second Amendment was not a fundamental constitutional right, and that legislative restrictions on the right did not require the Court to apply strict scrutiny review to the case, which, as you mentioned earlier, is a rigorous level of judicial scrutiny reserved only for restrictions on fundamental rights.

You may remember that the Supreme Court was asked to analyze this case in the context of gun ownership being a fundamental right. There are certain rights in the Constitution—such as freedom of speech, freedom of religion, freedom of the press—that are regarded as fundamental rights. Our fundamental constitutional rights are protected from governmental intrusion by the application of this very rigorous test of judicial review. This means that, in order for any federal restriction on a fundamental right to succeed in the courts, the restriction must be shown to serve a compelling interest of the federal government, it must be narrowly tailored in scope, and it must be shown to be effective in achieving the government's compelling interest. This is a very high level of scrutiny that the Court applies to government restrictions on a fundamental constitutional right.

On the other hand, the Supreme Court uses another standard of judicial review when determining the constitutionality of restrictions on rights that are not fundamental rights. This lower standard of judicial review is called rational basis scrutiny, because the standard that the Court applies to the restriction is a determination whether or not there is a rational basis for the government's restriction on whatever right might be at issue.

The fact that the Supreme Court applied rational basis scrutiny as opposed to strict scrutiny in the *Lewis* case leads to the conclusion that there is no fundamental right to keep and bear arms under the Second Amendment. The right that does exist under the Second Amendment—of the well-regulated state militias to keep and bear arms—is a constitutional right, but it is not one of the upper echelon fundamental rights.

In the federal courts, the fact that the Second Amendment does not provide a constitutional right to individuals to possess firearms is well settled. In the political arena, however, the meaning of the Second Amendment is very different. It is invoked to argue that gun control violates the Constitution. This argument is simply not accurate. The Second Amendment is also invoked by those who argue that gun control is evidence of a tyrannical government because, they claim, government restrictions on private gun ownership violate one of the fundamental constitutional rights. This argument is also inaccurate, as I just pointed out.

Let me point out another thing. Whatever restrictions the Second Amendment places on governmental activity only apply to the actions of the federal government. Unlike other rights found in the Constitution, the Second Amendment has never been held by the Supreme Court to restrict the conduct of states. So even if we were to find that somehow the federal government could not regulate private gun ownership—which it certainly can—but even if we were to find that it could not, the Second Amendment still allows the states full authority to restrict gun ownership.

The Supreme Court has found that the Fourteenth Amendment protects citizens not only from the infringements of rights by the federal government, but from the state governments as well. For instance, the Sixth Amendment right to a jury trial and the First Amendment right to freedom of speech have been held to apply to the states. However, the Second Amendment has never been held to apply to the states.

A.P. Is there any dissent in the case law that argues to the contrary of what you have just stated? In other words, is there any doubt in the courts that the Congress has the authority under the Constitution to enact gun-control laws?

B.L. There has never been a majority opinion in a federal case that suggests what you are asking. I would like to read for the record what some of these cases have said about this. These cases will show that the Second Amendment merely protects the right of the well-regulated militias of the states as instruments of state government. It does not protect private gun ownership.

For example, in the *Miller* case, the Supreme Court ruled as follows:

> In the absence of any evidence tending to show that possession or use of a [shotgun] at this time has some reasonable relationship to the preservation or efficiency of a well-regulated militia, we cannot say that the Second Amendment guarantees the right to keep and bear such an instrument.[14]

In the *Lewis* case, while quoting from *Miller,* the Supreme Court ruled as follows, while reviewing the constitutionality of the provisions in the 1968 federal Gun Control Act:

> These legislative restrictions on the use of firearms are neither based upon constitutionally suspect criteria, nor do they trench upon any constitutionally protected liberties.... The Second Amendment guarantees no right to keep and bear a firearm that does not have "some reasonable relationship to the preservation or efficiency of a well regulated Militia."[15]

In *United States v. Hale,* the U.S. Court of Appeals for the Eighth Circuit, while referring to *Miller,* stated:

Considering this history, we cannot conclude that the Second Amendment protects the individual possession of military weapons.... The rule emerging from *Miller* is that, absent a showing that the possession of a certain weapon has "some reasonable relationship to the preservation or efficiency of a well regulated militia," the Second Amendment does not guarantee the right to possess the weapon.[16]

The decision in *Hale* was rendered more than fifty years after *Miller*, so that should give you a sense of the uninterrupted precedent that *Miller* has set. And there have been many other federal cases on the Second Amendment in between. For example, in *Stevens v. United States*, the U.S. Court of Appeals for the Sixth Circuit stated:

Since the Second Amendment right "to keep and bear arms" applies only to the right of the state to maintain a militia, and not to the individual's right to bear arms, there can be no serious claim to any express constitutional right of an individual to possess a firearm.[17]

That is a pretty clear and definitive interpretation of the Second Amendment. Another important federal case was *United States v. Warin*, where the U.S. Court of Appeals for the Sixth Circuit turned away a Second Amendment challenge to a federal law requiring the registration of automatic weapons. In *Warin*, the Sixth Circuit stated that "[i]t is clear that the Second Amendment guarantees a collective right rather than an individual right," and referred to the "erroneous supposition that the Second Amendment is concerned with the rights of individuals rather than those of states."[18]

All of the federal cases on the Second Amendment and federal gun-control laws since *Miller*, and there are perhaps fifteen or twenty, have ruled that the amendment does not give private citizens the right to purchase or possess firearms. Likewise, there is no constitutional right to train with firearms, or to form a private army.

The National Rifle Association (NRA) and the militias do not recognize the courts' interpretation of the Second Amendment, either because they do not recognize the legitimacy of the federal judiciary, which is the case with many antigovernment extremists, or because they do not agree with the Supreme Court's interpretation in the *Miller* case.

The NRA and some militia groups interpret *Miller* as establishing constitutional protection for firearms that have a military function. The NRA has argued this point in its litigation efforts in Second Amendment cases. And you will find reference to this interpretation of *Miller* in some of the militia literature.

But this is clearly not what the *Miller* court contended in its ruling. And this is evident in the case law. In an important law review article on the Second Amendment, gun rights, and the meaning of constitutional references to the militia, Keith Ehrman and Dennis Henigan write that "[t]he proposition that *Miller* recognizes the protected status of any weapon that could have a military use has been rejected by every court which has addressed it." The authors write: "This argument seems absurd on its face, because it would accord constitutional protection to machine guns, bazookas, hand grenades, and other military hardware of staggering destructive potential."[19] Yet this is precisely the argument that the NRA and militia groups advance when they claim constitutional protection for these kinds of weapons.

In 1942, three years after the *Miller* case, the U.S. Court of Appeals for the First Circuit rejected a Second Amendment challenge to the 1938 Federal Firearms Act,[20] which prohibited fugitives and felons from transporting firearms in interstate commerce. In this case, *Cases v. United States,* the First Circuit, while referring to "distinctly military arms, such as machine guns, trench mortars, anti-tank or anti-aircraft guns," argued that "it would be inconceivable that a private person could have any legitimate reason for having such a weapon."[21] Ehrman and Henigan further observe: "The court in *Cases* also recognized that since some sort of military use seems to have been found for almost any modern lethal weapon, to read *Miller* to grant constitutional protection to all weapons of military potential would be to empower the federal government to regulate only weapons which can be classified as antiques or curiosities, such as the flintlock musket."[22]

The key to understanding the federal courts' interpretation of the Second Amendment lies in the nature of the debate at the Constitutional Convention between the Federalists, who favored a strong federal government, and the Anti-Federalists, who feared a strong federal government.

During the Constitutional Convention there were extensive debates about achieving the proper balance between federal and state power. One aspect of this debate concerned the status of the federal army, and whether it should be dissolved so as not to pose or seem to pose a threat to the security of the states and the regulated state militias, which, prior to the war, had been the traditional form of military organization in the colonies.

Ehrman and Henigan describe the debate at the Constitutional Convention:

> The key focus of the [Constitutional] Convention was this struggle over the proper roles of the federal government and the states. In the process, the rights of individual citizens rarely became an issue. Indeed, it was not until the end of the Convention that a proposal for a Bill of Rights was introduced.... Nowhere in the Constitutional debates was there a discussion of a right to keep or bear arms. The delegates at the Convention, however, did spend a good deal of time debating the roles of the army and militia, and these discussions are vital in understanding the Second Amendment.... In the context of the Constitution, the militia was viewed as a state-organized, state-run body, it was not simply a term for the citizenry at large.... The militias were seen as state units which could be armed by the government, and which could be called out by the states to quash rebellions, and defend the state from invasion.[23]

This is why the courts have never ruled that the Second Amendment gives private individuals a constitutional right to have a gun; the right given in the Second Amendment belongs to the state-organized, state-run military organizations—the "well-regulated militia" referenced in the Second Amendment, and which today is the National Guard pursuant to federal legislation.

The insurrectionist mission of the private militias of today is totally antithetical to the mission of the state-sponsored militias of the colonial period, which, in part, was to subdue armed insurrections against the state.

This idea that the Second Amendment gives private individuals the constitutional right to have firearms so as to be equipped to organize as private armies and threaten violence against the government comes in part from a relatively recent evolution of the NRA's interpretation of the Second Amendment. A handful of legal scholars as well have made this argument in law review articles that dissent from the judicial consensus on the meaning of the Second Amendment.

The most prominent scholar to argue that the Second Amendment gives private citizens the right to armed insurrection against the federal government is Professor Sanford Levinson, who published an article in the *Yale Law Journal*.[24]

Levinson argues that by creating an armed citizenry at large to be the militia, and by giving that right to individual citizens, the Second Amendment provides a right to armed opposition against a tyrannical government. This interpretation of the Second Amendment is known as the insurrectionist theory of the Second Amendment, and it is an interpretation that the NRA and the armed private militias subscribe to.

The insurrectionist theory suggests that the main purpose of the Second Amendment is to guarantee an individual right to gun ownership to counteract potential government tyranny. While there might be some cosmetic appeal to that interpretation, even among people who do not belong to a militia, it is a very dangerous theory that is antithetical to the purposes of the Constitution and to our democracy. It probably has its roots, not in the Constitution, but in the Declaration of Independence, which talked about the right of people to rise up against a tyrannical government.

However, our Constitution provides institutional and procedural checks and balances, and also establishes individual freedoms as fundamental rights, to legally and peacefully prevent the formation of a tyrannical government. We have three branches of government—legislative, executive, and judicial—with no single branch being superior or totally unaccountable to the others. And we have a Bill of Rights that protects individuals from government encroachment.

This constitutional framework is a magnificent and brilliant charter for the governance of a free people. However, it requires vigilance on the part of its citizens. In too many cases in our country today, this vigilance is lacking. And in the militia movement, there are no doubt some sincere people who believe that they are providing the kind of vigilance required to maintain our Constitution against government tyranny. But they are misguided when they claim rights that do not exist in the Constitution, or propose a right to citizen violence that is outside the Constitution. There simply is no right to armed insurrection in the Constitution. The belief in such a right poses a grave danger to the Constitution. And the very small handful of legal scholars and gun-rights lobbyists who are proposing the existence of a constitutional right to armed insurrection are perpetrating a dangerous fraud upon this country.

We should be asking advocates of the insurrectionist theory how this theory would be put into practice. Who is going to determine when the government has become tyrannical? What is the reach of the right in terms of the weapons that we are entitled to have? What are the parameters of this kind of armed engagement against the government? Do citizens really have a constitutional right to attack with military weapons the Supreme Court, or the Congress, or the White House, or federal buildings and federal employees? If this were really a constitutional right, wouldn't there be some guidance in the Constitution to help us answer these very disturbing questions?

Dennis Henigan is probably the leading litigator and writer in the country today on constitutional issues relating to firearms. This is what he had to say recently about Sanford Levinson's insurrectionist theory of the Second Amendment:

> And some serious questions need to be asked of someone like Levinson. For example if there is this constitutional right, and if it is individual in nature, does it encompass an individual's right to determine when government has gone too far? Who, in fact, is to determine when government has gone too far? Obviously, Levinson would not want government to determine that because that would defeat the right. So, if it is to be an individual right, in any meaningful sense, then I as an individual must have the constitutionally guaranteed right to decide when my government has gone too far and then to take up arms against it.
>
> Well, if that's where we are going with this, does that mean that I have the constitutional right to assassinate public officials if I believe in good faith that they have gone too far? Would the Ku Klux Klan have the constitutional right to attack public school officials who are trying to enforce desegregation because the Klan believed in good faith that that was tantamount to tyranny? I can't imagine any person taking that view of our Constitution, and yet it seems to me to be a view that is the logical extension of Levinson's theory of the Second Amendment, as well as the NRA's theory of the Second Amendment, and the logical extension of all of the rhetoric we hear about having the right to bear arms in order to resist tyranny.
>
> If this is seriously being suggested as a constitutional right, then these advocates, I believe, are sowing the seeds of anarchy in this country.[25]

As I mentioned, and as we read in Henigan, the NRA also puts forward this insurrectionist theory of the Second Amendment, and this view of the Second Amendment is behind the NRA's increasingly strident efforts to oppose even limited gun-control laws. Since no gun-control bill introduced or passed in the Congress would threaten to confiscate the firearms of law-abiding sportsmen, or of law-abiding citizens to defend themselves in their own homes, the NRA resorts to misinformation campaigns about the meaning of the Second Amendment and the tyranny of federal agencies that enforce gun control laws.

Many people are familiar with the "jack-booted thugs" letter that Wayne LaPierre of the NRA sent out as a fund-raiser, referring to agents of the Bureau of Alcohol, Tobacco, and Firearms (ATF). This is the agency that enforces federal firearms laws. But many people are not aware of the broader implications of the NRA's interpretation of the Second Amendment. For example, while endorsing Levinson's interpretation of the Second Amendment, LaPierre in his recent book signaled to others more extreme than himself that an armed insurrectionist movement in the United States is not as far-fetched as it might seem:

> The twentieth century provides no example of a determined populace with access to small arms having been defeated by a modern army. The Russians lost in Afghanistan, the United States lost in Vietnam and the French lost in Indo-China. In each case it was the poorly armed populace that beat the "modern" army.... Modern nations like Algeria, Angola, Ireland, Israel, Mozambique and Zimbabwe only exist because guerrilla warfare can triumph over modern armies.[26]

Both the NRA and the militias subscribe to the insurrectionist theory, both see gun control as a violation of fundamental individual liberties, and both see gun control as part of a nefarious government plot to disarm Americans. In an article in *The New York Times Magazine,* Tanya Metaksa of the NRA is quoted as saying that gun control is part of "a hidden agenda among what I call gun prohibitionists who want to disarm the American people."[27]

I am a gun owner myself, and I know how to use a firearm. And although I do not have a constitutional right to a firearm, I have a statutory right to a firearm, which, like many other Americans, I exercise responsibly. And I am confident that as long as I do not commit a felony or violent misdemeanor, I will be able to exercise this statutory right for the foreseeable future.

If you have not been convicted of a violent crime, and if you have a legitimate use for a firearm, either for sport or for self defense, then your access to a legal firearm for those purposes has not been denied by the Brady law or the assault weapons ban, and it will not be preempted by future gun laws.

A.P. If the insurrectionist theory were a legitimate constitutional theory, the attorneys for suspects in the bombing of the federal building in Oklahoma City could plausibly apply the theory as a legitimate defense. Suppose that some individuals viewed the government as a tyranny due, for example, to the passage of gun-control laws. If the insurrectionist theory were valid, these persons would have the right under the Second Amendment to attack federal targets as a legitimate expression of political dissent in the United States.

B.L. Look, we could go back quite far in our history and find that sedition and assassination and all of these kinds of things are criminalized. Even during or before the time when George Washington was president, armed rebellions were put down—the Whiskey Rebellion in 1794, for instance, as well as Shays Rebellion in 1786. There is simply no basis, either in history, law, or logic, for this insurrectionist theory. But you are right; it does have these profound implications which some people in the militia movement are beginning to act out.

The insurrectionist interpretation of the Second Amendment by the NRA and others has permitted the militias to make a variety of bogus claims. For example, the militias claim that gun control violates their fundamental constitutional rights under the Second Amendment. This false belief is behind the militia view that the Brady bill and the assault weapons ban constitute federal infringement of a fundamental right, and in this way threatens tyranny.

The militias also see their existence justified by the Second Amendment in the sense that the amendment provides for the establishment of a well-regulated militia. The militias point to their command structure and training and say that they are well regulated. Actually, the more organized and well-trained an armed militia group is, the more likely it will be that they are engaged in illegal organizing and training.

The militias also believe that they have a constitutional right to conduct paramilitary training because this is consistent with their supposed right to keep and bear arms and with their preparations as an armed counterweight to federal authority.

The notion of a constitutional right to paramilitary training was expressed during the course of hearings on the militias conducted last fall in the Subcommittee on Crime of the House Judiciary Committee. I was one of the analysts invited to speak at those hearings. Another invited analyst was David Kopel of the Cato Institute. Here is what Kopel said about the right to paramilitary training:

> The Southern Poverty Law Center has begun promoting a federal ban on group firearms training, which is not authorized by state law. But state governments are perfectly capable of banning or authorizing whatever they want. The proposal for a federal ban amounts to asking Washington for legislation which the majority of states have already rejected. The right to keep and bear arms necessarily includes the right to practice with them, just as the constitutional right to read a newspaper editorial about political events necessarily includes the right to learn how to read in a group, and that group happens to promote incorrect political beliefs.[28]

This statement shows how the claim that the Second Amendment gives people the right to own a gun can mushroom into claims of constitutional protection for paramilitary training and military organizing.

As I was flipping through the transcript pages to read you that quote, I came across another statement by Kopel, where he endorses the idea of paramilitary training in the context of his own informal exposition of the insurrectionist theory:

> There's nothing wrong in this country with owning a gun. And any analysis of the history of our Second Amendment shows that it wasn't written so that people could go skeet shooting, it was written to protect the balance of power in a free society so that just as information power is diffused throughout society by the First Amendment or property power is diffused by the Fifth Amendment, physical force power is not a government monopoly. And that's the ultimate point of the Second Amendment. It used to be considered a very honorable, positive thing for groups to get together in voluntary organizations and train how to do their duty as citizens, which includes the civil defense of society, just as much [as] their duty may be to serve on a jury or in another collective capacity. The collective military training, collective training in the use of firearms, is something we ought to be encouraging, not discouraging.[29]

If, in his remarks, Kopel was referring to the National Guard, today's modern militia established by federal legislation, then these remarks would have been appropriate. But this statement was made at congressional hearings on armed civilian militias, and in this context, these remarks clearly misinterpret the meaning of the Second Amendment. And I would say that his support for militia training as an important civic duty is misguided.

Although citizens are free to organize to oppose government policies, there is no constitutional right for a citizens' organization to possess firearms. This does not mean that individual militia members cannot legally possess firearms. And if a group legally possesses firearms, then they do have a constitutional right to associate if they are not a military organization. But this is totally different from arguing that an individual or a group has a constitutional right to possess firearms and to organize as a private military force. Such rights simply do not exist under the Constitution.

So we should distinguish between rights that are granted by the Constitution, and rights that exist under statutory law. What this means is that the legality of firearms possession by militia members is governed by applicable federal and state laws, not the Constitution. For example, the purchase and possession of automatic weapons—machine guns—is prohibited by federal law. Thus, any militia member in possession of a machine gun would be violating federal law. And any militia member who purchases an assault weapon prohibited by the assault weapons ban would be in violation of federal law. However, a militia member who possesses a firearm in compliance with federal law legally possesses that firearm. But he does not have a right to use that firearm for paramilitary training, and he can be prevented from using a firearm for such training if state or federal law prohibits paramilitary training.

The fact that the Second Amendment does not guarantee individuals a constitutional right to a firearm does not mean that firearms cannot be legally purchased or owned. What it does mean is that the legal status of firearms possession is subject to federal and state laws, and the extent to which the government constrains or permits firearms possession is legitimately determined by the legislative and executive branches of the government. To put it more simply, the Second Amendment does not prevent the enactment of federal or state gun-control laws. But citizens can still retain a right to firearms possession through statutory law and under state constitutions so long as they do not conflict with federal provisions. This right is likely to be limited and regulated, but such regulations reflect the government's interest in public safety, and not some clandestine government conspiracy to disarm the country for the purpose of an armed takeover by whomever.

A.P. Kopel appears to argue that armed civilian militias are constitutionally protected groups, and that paramilitary training is a constitutionally protected activity. What are the court cases involving the constitutional status of armed civilian militias and paramilitary training?

B.L. The controlling Supreme Court case ruling on the status of private armies and military training is *Presser v. Illinois*,[30] an 1886 case. In this case the Supreme Court upheld the authority of the state of Illinois to ban private military organizations.

Remember that we mentioned before how the Second Amendment has never been applied to limit states. Based on this fact, *Presser* is still good law and has never been overturned. Let me quote a key passage from the *Presser* ruling:

> The right voluntarily to associate together as a military company or organization, or to drill or parade with arms, without and independent of an Act of Congress or law of the State authorizing the same, is not an attribute of national citizenship. Military organization and military drill and parade under arms are subjects especially under the control of the government of every country. They cannot be claimed as a right independent of law. Under our political system they are subject to the regulation and control of the State and Federal Governments, acting in due regard to their respective prerogatives and powers. The Constitution and laws of the United States will be searched in vain for any support to the view that these rights are privileges and immunities of citizens of the United States independent of some specific legislation on the subject.[31]

The *Presser* case is key to our statutory remedies banning militia organizing and training, and its ruling places civilian militias as well as paramilitary training outside the protections of the Constitution.

At the Southern Poverty Law Center, our founder, Morris Dees, litigated a case in the 1980s called *Vietnamese Fishermen's Association v. Knights of the Ku Klux Klan,*[32] in which the opinion cited *Presser* as the precedent for its ruling.

The Klan in Texas had created their own private army, which was intimidating and terrorizing Vietnamese fishermen in Galveston Bay. These Vietnamese had emigrated to the United States after the Vietnam War. The case was a civil action, and the Klan was enjoined from harassing and intimidating Vietnamese fishermen in the exercise of their civil rights, which in this case included fishing in Galveston Bay.

The court also enjoined the Klan from operating a private paramilitary army in Texas in violation of Texas law. The court in this case ruled that "Texas has the power to regulate the formation of private armies and such regulation does not violate either [the] First or Second Amendments." It also said that its "[i]njunction against a private association's military activities does no violence to the Second Amendment" and that "[t]he Second Amendment does not imply any general constitutional right for individuals to bear arms and form private armies."[33]

The federal district court in Houston in the *Vietnamese Fishermen* case cited *Presser* as the Supreme Court precedent in this area, and also cited a ruling in the 1940s by a New York State appellate court in a case involving an armed civilian militia in New York. In *Application of Cassidy*,[34] the New York court ruled as follows, as excerpted by the federal court in *Vietnamese Fishermen*:

> There can be no justification for the organization of such
> an armed force. Its existence would be incompatible with
> the fundamental concept of our form of government. The
> inherent potential danger of any organized private militia,
> even if never used or even if ultimately placed at the dis-
> posal of the government, is obvious. Its existence would be
> sufficient, without more, to prevent a democratic form of
> government, such as ours, from functioning freely, with-
> out coercion, and in accordance with the constitutional
> mandates.[35]

These three cases—*Presser, Vietnamese Fishermen,* and *Application of Cassidy*—show that the Second Amendment does not protect the formation and existence of private armies, and is not a barrier to legislation banning private armies and paramilitary training.

A.P. In fact, many states have enacted laws banning private armies, paramilitary training, or both, yet we have militias organizing in every state in the union, and militias conducting paramilitary training in nearly every state in the union. To my knowledge no state that has these laws on the books has enforced these statutes to prosecute members of a private army or those engaged in paramilitary training.

B.L. As you mentioned, there are basically two types of statutes that address militia organizing and paramilitary training. Anti-paramilitary laws generally prohibit private paramilitary training with weapons or explosives when carried out with the knowledge or intent that the training will be used to further a civil disorder, acts of violence, or violations of the law.

Anti-militia laws are a little different. These laws do not have the same kind of intent requirement. They merely require a showing that a group of people are associated together in a formal military-style organization. Anti-militia laws do not require a showing that any violence will necessarily come about as a result of the militia organizing.

A.P. It seems clear that *Presser* establishes the constitutionality for these kinds of statutes. Yet, in his excellent book on the militia movement, Kenneth Stern writes: "[S]ome states' attorneys general are worried about possible constitutional problems with the [anti-militia and anti-paramilitary training] laws on their books."[36] What is the concern among these attorneys general about the constitutionality of these statutes?

B.L. Both statutes addressing paramilitary training and militia organizing are constitutional. Some state attorneys general just might not be familiar with them. Still others may believe, as some state and federal officials do, that the Second Amendment protects militias and paramilitary training. In fact, there is no case law on the books right now that would directly support a Second Amendment challenge to any of the state anti-paramilitary training laws or anti-militia statutes. In any event, as I have mentioned, the Second Amendment does not restrict state action, so no state attorney general would be constrained by the Second Amendment anyway from prosecuting groups engaged in paramilitary training with the intent of committing a civil disorder or organizing as a private army.

   A.P. What about the constitutionality of these statutes under the First Amendment?

   B.L. The First Amendment does not protect the right of people to assemble with the intent of committing a civil disorder. It protects "the right of the people *peaceably* to assemble." And *Presser* has ruled that private armies are not protected by the Constitution. The government often regulates associational relationships. Marriages, dwelling occupancy, and professional licensing are a few examples of regulated associations. So neither the First Amendment nor the Second Amendment bars states from prosecuting individuals under the statutes that prohibit paramilitary training and militia organizing.

   If you want to split hairs, as between the two types of statutes, the paramilitary training statutes are regarded as marginally more insulated from constitutional attack than the militia statutes. This is for two reasons. First, there is a federal analog to the state paramilitary training statutes—the Civil Disobedience Act of 1968,[37] the constitutionality of which has been consistently upheld. This law prohibits a person from instructing another in paramilitary techniques with the intent of fomenting a civil disorder.

   The problem with these statutes for government officials might lie in the kind of thinking reflected by David Kopel in his statement that "the right to keep and bear arms necessarily includes the right to practice with them." We have already observed that the Supreme Court in the *Miller* case ruled that there is no constitutional right for a private individual to have a firearm, and that the Court ruled in the *Presser* case that there is no right in the Constitution to organize or train as a private army. So there is a major flaw in Kopel's argument in light of the Supreme Court's rulings in these two cases.

   There is, however, one legitimate constitutional concern with these statutes that needs to be addressed. When the government bans private armies and paramilitary training through the enactment of these statutes, it cannot target groups for proscription because it does not like what they are saying. This is not a legitimate basis for proscribing militia organizing and training. With these statutes the government can target militias, but not because it finds their antigovernment rhetoric repulsive. Rather, it targets them because of the dangers private armies pose to a democratic society—because of the inherent risk to societal order in having private military bodies with sophisticated military-type weapons unanswerable to any kind of governmental authority.

Thus, it does not matter that these armed groups advocate ideas that are repulsive to some people or to the government; armed militias might come along some day and advocate ideas that the majority of Americans might find attractive. The point is, I would advocate banning them in both instances because of the inherent incompatibility between democracy and constitutionalism on the one hand, and private armies outside of government regulation on the other. And because of the inherent threat posed by private armies, the government has a compelling state interest to bring these bodies under its regulatory authority. But the government has a responsibility to enforce these kinds of laws in a content-neutral manner, and cannot target groups for selective enforcement because it does not like the ideas that the groups are expressing.

Let me mention another point, this time going back to the First Amendment. The First Amendment protects freedom of association, and it protects the expression of ideas—even unpopular ideas. But it does not protect the right of individuals to gather at any time and in any manner in which they see fit. The First Amendment's guarantees apply to the right of people to peaceably assemble and to petition the government for redress of grievances, and the First Amendment most vigorously protects those associations that involve the peaceful expressions of political ideas. Anti-paramilitary and anti-militia laws clearly do not violate the First Amendment because they restrict military associations and activities, not speech or political pursuits. And that is why the courts have upheld these kinds of laws.

We would do well to go back and read *Presser, Vietnamese Fishermen,* and *Application of Cassidy.* These are very eloquent and powerful statements regarding the fundamental incompatibility of having private armies in a democracy. We would do well indeed as a nation to use these opinions as our guide in developing legislative remedies to address the proliferation of these armed groups.

A.P. So the anti-militia and anti-paramilitary training statutes developed by the Southern Poverty Law Center would apply not only to armed right-wing militias, but to any group of private citizens who wanted to form their own private army, irrespective of their politics.

B.L. That's right. Also, we have to look at a couple of problems definitionally. Many groups that might call themselves militias might not be breaking militia laws. So you have to look at the characteristics of the group in order to determine its legal status. A few people getting together to shoot at a target in the woods without the requisite intent, or without really being an assembled private military army, would not be engaging in conduct or associations in violation of these statutes.

A.P. What kind of activity would likely be banned by a federal anti-militia statute?

B.L. It would basically ban the creation and maintenance of private military organizations.

A.P. How would a law enforcement official distinguish between a private military organization and a few people gathered together in the woods shooting at a target? How would the statute be enforced?

B.L. The criminal law looks at the situational nexus of activities all the time. For instance, if I use a screw driver to break into your home, that is possession of burglar's tools. But having a screw driver in and of itself is not a crime. So what you have to do is look at the characteristics of the organization, what they are doing, and what their apparent intent is.

One of the things that we would look for in identifying a military organization is whether the group operates under a command structure, because a command structure is an attribute of a military organization that would help us distinguish between a private army or militia and a group of people gathering for target practice. Other things that you would have to look at are whether the group consists of soldiers or armed persons, whether they drill with weapons in a particular way, and whether they are reasonably capable of being assembled for unified independent service in an armed conflict.

To address your enforcement question, these laws are not that easy to enforce. They are by no means prohibitively difficult, but they are not easy. You have to prove beyond a reasonable doubt that people are gathering together as a military body. And certainly how they conduct themselves, and what their intentions are, are all relevant in coming to that determination. But a prosecutor would still have significant proof problems to overcome.

A.P. Suppose in response to the enactment of anti-militia and anti-training laws, the militias reorganize themselves into leaderless cells, which are essentially armed underground terrorist groups with no apparent command structure. Some militia groups have already reorganized themselves in this way. How could the law be structured to protect the public from the threat of violence posed by these underground armed groups? Could you describe what these leaderless resistance groups are, and how the legal system might address this threat?

B.L. Leaderless resistance is a way of organizing that has been put forth most recently by white supremacist and militia leaders, and which creates small autonomous groups of armed individuals poised to commit random acts of sabotage and terrorism. They are not part of an organized command and control structure per se. They do whatever they like, separate from any chain of command or authority, to inflict damage or injury to infrastructure targets or innocent citizens.

This is more difficult to address by any single new statute. Certainly to the extent that they engage in paramilitary training they would violate paramilitary training statutes. To the extent that they plan to commit criminal acts, they would violate conspiracy statutes. If they are seeking to overthrow the government, they would be in violation of treason statutes. So there are a variety of traditional laws that they probably would be breaking, in addition to perhaps operating in violation of a paramilitary training statute or even a militia statute.

What you hope to do with these various statutes is to have several laws that can be applied in a number of situations. First, I would want to apply these militia statutes to get at those groups that are in fact militias because their presence poses a threat and intimidates people. I would also want to have a paramilitary statute at the same time, to address paramilitary training. And where a conspiracy to overthrow the government exists, statutes dealing with conspiracy, treason, and sedition can serve as a basis for prosecution. Also, there is a rarely used law involving foreknowledge that someone else is going to commit a crime. This is called misprison of a felony. And if someone transports or possesses weapons and explosives in a certain manner, he can be prosecuted under certain statutes as well. I will include the citations of these statutes in the appendix.

What I am saying is that we are not merely limited to the application of the anti-militia and anti-paramilitary training laws in dealing with the proliferation of militia groups and underground terrorist cells. But certainly the anti-militia and anti-paramilitary training laws are part of an overall framework for state and federal prosecutors in deterring and preventing violent activity.

A.P. For the purposes of enforcing some of these statutes, what is the difference between target practice and paramilitary training?

B.L. Target practice usually involves stationary target practice, and military training involves instruction of an array of violent techniques. However, I would argue that if someone got together with another person and conducted target practice, and they intended to use that target practice to foment a civil disorder, and you could prove that in court, then technically you might be able to prosecute that person. But that is a proof problem.

A lot of the paramilitary training statutes rely on being able to show that the techniques, the weaponry, the situation, and the intent all point to fomenting violence and civil disorder. But if you are just shooting at a target, and you are doing it for recreational or sporting purposes, the government is not going to be able to prove that you had this intent to foment a civil disorder.

The criminal law consistently looks at your intent; in other words it looks at what your purpose and knowledge were in conducting an activity. So you have to look at the intent of the person, and you also have to look at what facts independently corroborate the intent that you might be trying to prove.

A.P. In terms of dealing with an underground terrorist cell, such as these leaderless cells, how would the government discover those facts? What authority does the federal government have to investigate or infiltrate these underground groups to determine whether or not they are engaged in criminal activity?

B.L. Let me make sure that I state this correctly. The federal guidelines suggest that there would have to be evidence that would reasonably indicate that two or more people are engaged in an enterprise for the purposes of furthering political or social goals involving force or violence in violation of the criminal laws of the United States.

In other words you need to have some kind of credible indication that a violation of federal law is going to take place. But if you have a federal anti-militia law on the books, then that gives you a basis right there for investigation because an underground terrorist cell would be an illegal military group under that statute. So another reason for enacting anti-militia statutes would be to allow federal investigation of, and to address the threat of, leaderless cells.

A.P. Let me go back to the enforcement issue regarding the anti-militia and anti-paramilitary training laws that are on the books already in a number of states. Twenty-four states currently have laws banning private armies. And we now have militias operating in every state in the union. But, to my knowledge, these laws are not being enforced in those states.

We have so much evidence that private armies are operating in states with anti-militia statutes. We have numerous press reports, we have admissions from militia officials that they are leaders or members of armed militia groups, where they call themselves militias and train as militias and threaten violence against a tyrannical government while citing their constitutional rights as militias.

What is the problem in terms of enforcement that has caused these states not to enforce their own laws?

B.L. Some state officials are not informed as to the existence of these laws, or as to the existence of militias in their states. And in some states you have problems with regard to officials not executing the laws the way that they should.

But in defense of many prosecutors, there are often significant problems relating to proof. You have to show that these people are organized as a private army, but a lot of militias will say they are merely an informational service or a political group.

A.P. Suppose you go out and photograph people dressed in camouflage military uniforms with assault weapons, an observable command structure, and an apparent or obvious training routine. These kinds of characteristics and activities do not seem to be unusual among the militia groups. There seems to be a surplus of evidence showing that these groups are organized and training as private armies.

B.L. Let me just respond for a second to your previous question. I would say that these laws are vastly under-enforced, but not necessarily due to malevolence on the part of prosecutors. Although we have had private armies around for some time, the way they exist now is a relatively new phenomenon. Also, I think in many places local authorities might be intimidated by these groups, and many of these militia groups have not committed the kind of overt activities that would cause them to come under the scrutiny of local authorities.

Contrary to what you just said in terms of the abundance of evidence concerning private armies, it is very difficult to get information about what people are doing. The fact that someone is dressed in camouflage and has a rifle is not in and of itself an indication of a criminal act. We need to be very careful not to tread on the rights of innocent people.

One thing that is important to remember about this movement is that there is a broad range of activity within it. Much of this activity is benign. A lot of the people that we are talking about are merely getting together, getting dressed in camouflage, doing target practice, and giving themselves some kind of title. I don't think that on that end of the spectrum, you will find many prosecutors jumping over hurdles to prosecute those individuals.

But, as I said, there is a spectrum, and some of these militia groups are very dangerous. And if there is an anti-militia law in a state, and if the state prosecutors are in possession of the kind of evidence necessary for conviction, then they should prosecute these groups.

A.P. In other words, in order for a private army to be prosecuted under the anti-militia statute, it would not only have to be organized as a private army, but it would have to do something belligerent to get the attention of a prosecutor, perhaps issue threats to a government official?

B.L. No. If you have a private army in a state that has an anti-militia statute, and the members of that army merely associate together as an organized body—they do not even have to train—that is a crime. And that is punishable.

I think though that there is a problem with regard to evidence. And that is, the association of a bunch of people in uniform with weapons does not make an army for the purposes of a criminal conviction. You would have to show that they are a military-type body. And certainly an association of people with weapons is probative of that. But if some good ol' boys dress up in camouflage, even if it is together in a group, without some other kind of corroborating evidence that this group is a private army or militia, it is insufficient to establish the violation of an anti-militia statute.

As a former police officer I can tell you that there are many factors that come into play that make enforcement of laws that are on the books difficult. We just covered evidentiary problems. But there is also a problem in the sense that in many states these laws have not been tested very much. Law enforcement officers may not be familiar with them. Given the way that many of these groups operate, the prosecutors may not know that they exist. Also, many times in the hierarchy of criminal activity, these prosecutors might feel that they would have a stronger case in court if they waited for some kind of more overt activity. In many instances, frankly, there is an intimidation factor.

I think that you will start to see more prosecutions as the threat of these groups becomes more apparent, and as prosecutors become more familiar with the tools that they have to address this threat.

There is also a resources factor that you have to keep in mind. Does a local law enforcement agency want to escalate a situation that it might be unable to control without significant risk of harm to officers or prosecutors? There are a variety of factors involved here in terms of when and how to enforce these statutes.

A.P. Doesn't your last point highlight the need for a federal anti-militia statute, which would bring the resources of the federal government to bear on the problem? This way state and local law enforcement agencies would not feel so intimidated and overwhelmed in terms of resources.

B.L. I think there are a variety of reasons why a federal anti-militia law is appropriate, not the least of which is what you just mentioned. But in addition, the federal government has an interest in the preservation of civil order, the protection of interstate commerce, the maintenance of the stability of the federal government, and the safety of federal officials. All of these things bring an anti-militia law totally within the domain of federal authority.

A.P. With the exception of your very last point, I have to say that I am surprised to hear you list all of these problems that stand in the way of prosecuting private armies under the anti-militia and anti-paramilitary training statutes in these states. By no means am I saying that we should prosecute people who do not violate the law, and I am not saying that all of these militia groups are dangerous. However, having said that, your boss, Morris Dees, commenting on the need to remedy the threat of militia violence, stated: "The problem with the [anti-militia and anti-paramilitary training] laws is that they have almost never been enforced. States with laws against militias or paramilitary training should vigorously enforce them. States without such laws should enact them."[38]

Your answers seem to back off from that a little bit. You seem to emphasize the problems with enforcing these laws. But one might also underscore the problems with not enforcing them.

B.L. I am in complete agreement with Morris Dees on this issue. I think there is a big problem with not enforcing these laws, which is that individuals within these private armies will become emboldened by the lack of enforcement. They will take nonenforcement as a tacit sign of approval for their activities, which are at the very least intimidating, and at the most represent a serious potential threat of violence and a threat to democracy. Their stated purpose, their access to sophisticated military weapons, and the fact that they train for violent actions pose a significant threat to orderly democracy. And many militia members talk openly of resorting to the cartridge box instead of the ballot box. And I think that the implementation of that course of action through militaristic organizing is dangerous and should be dealt with firmly, squarely, and unambiguously when appropriate.

A.P. How would the federal government do that—if it enacts an anti-militia statute and modifies its anti-training statute—when faced with the problems of enforcement that you have been itemizing? What is the recourse of the federal government to respond to this threat given the enforcement problems?

B.L. There are enforcement and evidentiary problems with prosecuting individuals under nearly every criminal law, and that is how it should be in a free society, because this constrains the government from incarcerating people at random. But just because I point out legitimate issues that need to be dealt with in terms of enforcement and evidence does not mean that states should not be enforcing these laws. As I have mentioned, the statutory remedies to this problem at the federal level are clear, and the statutes that need to be enacted would be constitutional and enforceable.

To facilitate the federal response to the threat of armed militias, I mentioned earlier that the federal government has to amend the federal anti-paramilitary training law to apply not only to paramilitary instructors, but to those receiving the instruction. The government should also enact an anti-militia law that would prohibit mere organization of a private army.

The federal government should also coordinate the monitoring of domestic terrorism, and work more closely with local authorities to address domestic terrorism. It also has to look toward preventing active-duty military personnel and law enforcement officials from engaging in these kinds of groups and activities.

The key items, however, in proposing legislative remedies in response to the threat posed by private armies is for states that do not already have them to enact both anti-militia and anti-paramilitary training statutes, and for the federal government to amend its current statute on paramilitary training to include trainees as well as instructors, and to enact the federal anti-militia statute as well.

These statutes, both existing and proposed, are constitutional, they do not infringe on legitimate constitutional rights, and they would serve the government's interest in maintaining civil order and protecting democratic institutions from the threat of violence posed by extremist antigovernment groups.

In the appendix I will reproduce the model anti-militia and anti-paramilitary training statutes from the Southern Poverty Law Center, and the anti-paramilitary training statute from the Anti-Defamation League. I also will list the militia and paramilitary training statutes already introduced by Congressman Jerrold Nadler.

A.P. I wanted to ask you about two other components of the antigovernment movement where constitutional and legal issues are implicated: the county supremacy movement, and the proliferation of common law courts. The basic idea behind the county supremacy movement is that the county, not the federal government, is the highest legal authority in the country.

B.L. The concept that state or county laws can trump federal law is just not found in the Constitution; in fact, the situation is quite the contrary. Article VI, section 2 of the Constitution, known as the Supremacy Clause, is unambiguously clear about federal authority, and makes federal law the supreme law of the land in the United States. So there is no constitutional basis for claiming that county law is supreme.

In addition, the jurisprudence under the Supremacy Clause has said that in the event of a conflict, state law must at all times yield to federal law. This is called preemption.

There are two instances where preemption actually comes into play. One is called "actual conflict," where there is clear and direct actual conflict between a federal statute and a state statute. And in those instances, the federal law simply preempts state law. The other instance is called "conflicting objectives," where even if on their faces these laws do not directly conflict, it would be impossible to comply with both. Here, the federal law or regulation stands.

There is a circumstance where the federal courts will allow a state law or county law to stand in the face of a federal law. This happens when a state or county law supplements a federal law. So for instance, if there is a federal antidiscrimination law, then there can be a similar state law. Obviously, there can be state and local laws regulating areas where the federal law is silent.

A.P. Individuals and groups involved in the county supremacy movement have litigated against the federal government over control of federal land. This has occurred mostly in the West, in such states as New Mexico and Nevada. Often local ranchers will challenge federal environmental laws or land-use regulations on federal lands. What is the constitutional argument behind these challenges to the jurisdiction of the federal government over federally owned lands?

B.L. To answer your question precisely I would need to know the specific situation as it applied to specific counties and specific federal lands. But I can answer your question generally. In general, where the federal government has ownership of land, the federal government certainly can decide how that land is used. Even in instances where the county owns land, the county can be constrained by federal regulation. For instance, let us say that the county wants to open a toxic waste dump, and there is a federal law that deals with how toxic materials are disposed of. The federal government can prevent the county government from using that land in a manner that violates federal law.

But there are obviously limits. The federal government certainly does not have the right to bulldoze city hall. The federal government, in fact, is also constrained by the Constitution. It cannot take property without due process, for example. But much of this tension comes about where the government basically licenses private individuals to use government land in a certain way—for example, licensing ranchers to have cattle graze in a certain area. But the federal government, just like any other landowner, has the right to relinquish a license if it chooses for reasons having to do with inappropriate use or violations of the conditions of the license.

In March 1996, Nye County in Nevada lost a court case against the federal government involving its claim to control federal land. This claim is a recent episode in Nevada's so-called Sagebrush Rebellion, which began in 1979 after the Nevada legislature passed laws claiming control over all public lands in Nevada. In 1993 Nye County passed a similar resolution, the legality of which was just rejected.

About three dozen other western counties in the United States are challenging the authority of federal agencies to enforce regulations on federal land. But, generally, these claims have no constitutional merit.

A.P. Many antigovernment extremists argue that U.S. membership in the United Nations is treasonous, for reasons which are not clear to me; but this is a common charge. Referring again to the Supremacy Clause of the U.S. Constitution, which also makes duly-ratified treaties the law of the land in the United States, how would you respond?

B.L. Given the provision of the Supremacy Clause that addresses treaties, and given that the U.N. Charter is a treaty that was signed by the president of the United States and ratified by the U.S. Senate in accordance with the ratification requirements of the Constitution, U.S. membership in the United Nations is not treasonous. Our membership in the United Nations is fully and legally valid under the Constitution. There isn't any question among legal scholars about this.

But many antigovernment extremists argue that U.S. membership in the United Nations is an infringement on the sovereignty of the United States, and on the rights of American citizens. Basically, however, a treaty is similar in force to federal law. If a state law or county law conflicts with a treaty, that state or county law will have to yield. But a treaty cannot take away someone's constitutional guarantees, such as freedom of speech or religion, or the right to vote. So our membership in the United Nations is not treasonous, and the Constitution prevents the United Nations or any other international body from infringing on the fundamental rights of American citizens on American soil.

A.P. Earlier you mentioned that the Declaration of Independence is a source of inspiration for antigovernment extremists. And in the context of talking about what motivates people to join leaderless resistance cells and prepare for a war of insurrection against the federal government, one could read the Declaration of Independence to find this inspiration. For example, here is what it reads in part:

> That whenever any Form of Government becomes destructive of these ends, it is the right of the People to alter or abolish it, and to institute new Government, laying its foundation on such principles, and organizing its powers in such form, as to them shall seem most likely to effect their Safety and Happiness.

Here is another sentence from the Declaration of Independence:

> But when a long train of abuses and usurpations, pursuing invariably the same Object, evinces a design to reduce them under absolute Despotism, it is their right, it is their duty, to throw off such Government, and to provide new Guards for their future security.

Is there any evidence that antigovernment extremists are inspired by these words from the Declaration of Independence?

B.L. Yes, and I think that they use it to give a veneer of credibility to their cause. The Declaration of Independence addresses the tyrannical English government's treatment of the colonies, and the grievances cited in the Declaration began the process that led to our Constitution, which contains the checks and balances and the protections that the colonists did not have to protect them from government abuse.

A.P. Does the Declaration of Independence confer any rights to individuals—a right to revolution or any other right?

B.L. No. The Declaration of Independence confers no rights or privileges to any citizen today. It is a very important document historically, in the sense that it effected our dissolution from the Crown. For this reason it is very significant. But the Constitution, not the Declaration of Independence, is the document from which all laws and rights in this country receive their validity.

A.P. So if a militia group cites the two passages of the Declaration of Independence that I just read to you as their legal basis for seeking to overthrow the federal government, that is no legal basis from which to proceed to attempt to do that.

B.L. Absolutely not. But I think that their claim to overthrow the government, when they cite the Declaration of Independence, is more of a philosophical claim than a legal one. They more often cite the Second Amendment as the basis for their legal right to overthrow the government. But even in the philosophical realm, it is an illegitimate claim. The remedy to the grievances found in the Declaration of Independence is the Constitution. The Constitution is the lawful framework in which the grievances listed in the Declaration were remedied. All of our laws, institutions, and procedures by which we govern ourselves today, reside and rest in the Constitution.

A.P. I wanted to ask you about the proliferation of common law courts. Would it be accurate to say that, if the armed militia movement is the military or paramilitary wing of the antigovernment movement, then the common law courts movement is the "judicial" wing of the antigovernment movement?

B.L. I think that is a fairly accurate description of the role of common law courts in the antigovernment movement. In some instances they are nothing more than sounding boards for individuals or groups in the movement. But in some areas I think they represent a significant threat.

Again, we are talking about a spectrum of ideologies and behaviors. But certainly, at a minimum, the idea that individuals are vesting authority in themselves to punish others under the force of law is not something that we can tolerate in a civilized democratic society. We cannot have private judicial fiefdoms springing up across the country. This is anarchy, and obviously not representative of a legitimate judicial system.

A.P. A report on common law courts aired on National Public Radio on January 12 of this year. In that report, the NPR reporter stated: "The First Amendment guarantees common law courts the right to convene, but by law the courts may not attempt to enforce their rulings." Does the First Amendment guarantee common law courts the right to convene?

B.L. It depends on what their intent is when they convene. Certainly they have a First Amendment right to have a mock court hearing. But they have no right to require someone to appear before them, to try to impose their mandate on anyone, or otherwise assert that their hearings have the force of law.

To the extent that someone wants to make a political statement by conducting a parody of something, they can do that. People are permitted to do a lot of idiotic things. But if they try to enforce what they are doing, at that point they are involved in impersonating court officials. This is not permitted under the First Amendment.

A.P. Has there been an instance when a common law court has attempted to enforce its rulings?

B.L. Yes, there have been several instances, including courts that have issued rulings and threatened government officials.

A.P. I recall reading that some common law courts have empowered militias to arrest people indicted by their courts.

B.L. That would be clearly illegal. Anyone that issues a bogus arrest warrant, including such a warrant issued by a common law court, is certainly committing a crime. And someone who directs another to commit a criminal act, such as kidnapping or unlawful imprisonment, is committing a crime as well.

A.P. Would it be legal for a common law court to issue a subpoena to someone to testify?

B.L. That would be illegal too. If you impersonate a government official, or if you make a bogus legal instrument, that is generally a crime. Common law courts are prohibited by law from issuing subpoenas and warrants and things of that nature. One cannot legally concoct a false, pseudo-official document, and attempt to enforce it.

The First Amendment allows parody, criticism, mockery, and verbal disparagement of public officials. However, when you cross the line and engage in unofficial judicial proceedings that you attempt to enforce, that is not protected by the First Amendment.

There are sound reasons why this kind of activity is illegal and punishable. When a police officer arrests someone who is then charged with a crime and ultimately brought to trial, these law enforcement and judicial officers do so with the appropriate legal authority. If someone else performs these identical acts without this authority, it is kidnapping. Likewise, if a court of law sentences someone upon conviction to prison, it does so with the requisite legal authority. If someone other than a legitimate court sentences someone to prison and confines that person against their will, that is a crime. The reasons for these distinctions should be obvious to everyone.

"Proceedings" that resemble peaceful protest are protected. But attempts to enforce bogus judicial rulings that might arise out of this protest are definitely not protected.

A.P. Common law court proponents claim that the Constitution says that courts should be run by people, not judges and attorneys.

B.L. This is another constitutional fantasy. The Constitution mandates that the Supreme Court shall be the highest court in the land, and that the Congress can establish lower courts. Certainly states have the ability in our dual sovereign system to have their own courts. So this claim by common law courts adherents is unfounded.

A.P. Proponents of common law courts argue that their courts are legal because they are based on the Ten Commandments, the Magna Carta, the Declaration of Independence, and the Constitution—their version of it.

B.L. The Ten Commandments, the Magna Carta, and the Declaration of Independence are not legal instruments that convey any kind of legal authority. They are certainly meaningful historical and philosophical documents. But they are not legal instruments for our governmental system.

A.P. Is there a threat that militias or leaderless cells will engage in attacks against populated areas or federal facilities using biological or chemical agents as weapons?

B.L. Most emphatically there is this threat. Law enforcement faces a serious challenge in dealing with these groups because of the multifaceted nature of the threat. Traditionally, terrorists have preferred bombs. But recently we have seen plots involving the use of toxins and pathogens. We have seen antigovernment extremists in possession of ricin and other types of toxic substances, such as bubonic plague and cyanide. The manufacture and dissemination of these dangerous substances are outlined in the literature that permeates the antigovernment movement. Given the accessibility of these substances, and the threats to use them, I think we have a very serious problem on our hands.

In some respects, the federal government has recognized the increasing threat of domestic terrorism, including the use of chemical and biological toxins. For instance, on June 15 of last year, President Clinton convened a secret meeting in Washington of top officials to frame a response to the possibility of domestic terrorism. Sometime in spring 1996, the U.S. Senate is going to examine the threat of domestic terrorism in hearings involving chemical and biological weapons. There are current plans to address the threat of possible terrorist attacks in the subway systems of New York City and Washington D.C. In Los Angeles there was a drill at a hospital which simulated a response to a terrorist attack with a chemical toxin or biological pathogen in a hotel. The anthrax and ricin threats alone, if used against populations in major urban areas, is almost too horrifying to contemplate.

Let me talk about anthrax for a second. Anthrax is a virus that, if released through an aerosol disbursant in any major city, could result in hundreds of thousands of fatalities within days. So I think that we have to wake up and realize this could happen unless we begin to take some proactive measures to address this threat. For example, it is not impossible, or even that difficult, to gain possession of a small amount of anthrax. And even a very small amount of anthrax would be enough to cause the kinds of fatalities that I just described. So, clearly, we need to tighten up laws that govern the possession, transport, and controls on anthrax, ricin, and other pathogens and toxins.

But we still lack an appreciation of the threat that exists. There is a heavy and ingrained glorification of violence in this movement, and attacks on infrastructure targets, such as dams, power stations, transportation and communications systems, as well as symbolic targets, such as national monuments and landmarks, are glorified. And attacks on these kinds of targets have been attempted in some places. In other words the lifelines and national symbols of our country are vulnerable to very serious assault from domestic terrorists using either explosives or toxins.

In the book, *The Turner Diaries,* which Timothy McVeigh allegedly read avidly and sold at gun shows, infrastructure facilities and federal buildings were attacked by domestic terrorists. I do not think that it really takes a seer to realize that there are more bombers of federal buildings and infrastructure targets out there.

A.P. Have any antigovernment extremists resorted to or attempted attacks with biological or chemical agents?

B.L. Yes. In Minnesota, four members of a Patriots council were charged with an attempt to poison federal government officials with ricin, one of the most dangerous toxins known.

In November of 1995, a member of the Aryan Nations was convicted of ordering bubonic plague from a private laboratory, for which he paid only $240.

In Arkansas, a survivalist was charged with possessing 130 grams of ricin, which is enough to kill about fourteen hundred people. This man committed suicide shortly after his arrest.

In addition to incidents with these toxic agents, there were a number of bombing plots that took place throughout 1995. These plots involved federal buildings and other federal targets, but were thwarted by federal agents before these targets were actually attacked. It is almost inevitable, however, that some of these plots will not be prevented.

A.P. Would you describe in more detail what leaderless cells are? Is this leaderless underground movement a growing terrorist movement?

B.L. Yes, unequivocally so. Committing acts of terrorism is part of the ideology of these groups. This terrorist mission is glorified in *The Turner Diaries* and by Louis Beam, the former Klansman and now paramilitary activist. So, yes, the leaderless cells are terrorist organizations who are preparing to commit acts of terrorism in the United States.

A.P. What is the appeal of leaderless resistance for people who are involved in some way or other in the antigovernment movement? What do people hope to accomplish by organizing as terrorist cells and by committing acts of terrorism?

B.L. The idea of leaderless resistance is a growing part of the ideological culture of the antigovernment movement. It advocates taking things into your own hands and doing what you can to cause havoc to the government and its affiliated institutions and agencies.

There is also an important practical aspect to the leaderless cells. From a practical standpoint, leaderless cells insulate the overall movement from collective criminal or civil liability, and it also makes these small groups harder to detect and infiltrate by law enforcement.

In some respect, the leaderless cells are applying lessons learned by right-wing extremists from the downfall of the Ku Klux Klan.

The Klan was engaged in acts of violence for which many Klan leaders were held liable in both criminal and civil cases. In this situation, Klan leaders were not insulated from the violent actions of certain Klan groups, and many Klan leaders were imprisoned as a result of criminal cases, or put out of business as a result of civil lawsuits like the ones filed by the Southern Poverty Law Center.

A.P. There is extreme antigovernment activism on a political level today, as well as on a paramilitary level. Are antigovernment extremists becoming part of the political process in order to change the laws that would permit the kind of paramilitary activity that we have been describing? Do you see this being a potential problem, in terms of these people getting elected to office with the intent of making the law more militia-friendly?

B.L. Yes I do, and it is not merely a potential problem. We have people in office right now across the country who are supporting laws, advocated by militia members, that would legalize militia activity. Here in Alabama militia activists went to some state legislators and asked for passage of a bill that would have the effect of legalizing militia organizing and paramilitary training, and so far it has passed the House Judiciary Committee in the Alabama legislature. We do not know yet what the outcome of this effort will be, but there will almost certainly be similar efforts made by militia groups in the legislatures of other states.

On the federal level, there are some members of the current Congress, recently elected to office, who have demonstrated support for the extreme antigovernment agenda of militia groups. Political lobbying by fringe right-wing groups in the United States is perfectly legal, and the election of extreme right-wing members of Congress is obviously legal too. But we should understand that part of addressing the threat of militia violence includes informed involvement in the political sphere, not just the legal and law enforcement spheres.

A.P. What does the future look like in the United States in terms of domestic terrorism?

B.L. If you want to peer into the future, look at such things as the numerous terrorist attacks in the Middle East, the Tokyo subway attacks with poison sarin gas, and the terrorist attacks that have taken place in London, in addition to the bombing of the federal building in Oklahoma City. The question in my mind is not whether there will be additional brutal terror attacks in the United States, but when and where they will take place, and how bad they will be. The conditions that are present right now pose a serious threat of escalation of domestic terrorism in this country.

There is a genuine, sinking feeling from those of us in the policy area of this issue that, if we do not start enacting remedies to counter this threat, we will once again be witness to more incidents in our country like the bombing of the federal building in Oklahoma City. The statutory remedies that I have outlined will not give us a total capability to thwart domestic terrorists. But they do give critical legal tools to the government to protect civil order and prosecute militia groups when it is required.

Appendix A

States with Laws Prohibiting
Militias and Paramilitary Training

I. STATES WITH LAWS PROHIBITING BOTH MILITIAS AND
   PARAMILITARY TRAINING

Florida. FLA. STAT. ANN. ch. 870.06, 790.29.
Georgia. GA. CODE ANN. §§ 38-2-277, 16-11-150 to -152.
Idaho. IDAHO CODE §§ 46-802, 18-8101 to -1805.
Illinois. ILL. REV. STAT. ch. 1805, para. 94-95.
New York. N.Y. MIL. Law § 240.
North Carolina. N.C. GEN. Stat. §§ 127A-151, 14-288.20.
Rhode Island. R.I. GEN. LAWS §§ 30-12-7, 11-55-1 to -3.

II. STATES WITH LAWS PROHIBITING MILITIAS

Alabama. ALA. CODE § 31-2-125.
Arizona. ARIZ. REV. STAT. Ann. § 26-123.
Iowa. IOWA CODE § 29A.31.
Kansas. KAN. STAT. ANN. § 48-203.
Kentucky. KY. REV. STAT. Ann. § 38.440.
Maine. ME. REV. STAT. ANN. tit. 37-B, § 342.2.
Maryland. MD. CODE ANN. art. 65, § 35.
Massachusetts. MASS. GEN. L. ch. 33, § 129-132.
Minnesota. MINN. STAT. § 624.61.
Mississippi. MISS. CODE ANN. § 33-1-31.
Nevada. NEV. REV. STAT. § 203.080.
New Hampshire. N.H. REV. STAT. ANN. § 111:15.
North Dakota. N.D. CENT. CODE § 37-01-21.
Texas. TEX. GOV'T CODE ANN. § 431.010.
Washington. WASH. REV. CODE § 38.40.120.
West Virginia. W. VA. CODE § 15-1F-7.
Wyoming. WYO. STAT. § 19-1-106.

III. STATES WITH LAWS PROHIBITING PARAMILITARY TRAINING.

Arkansas. ARK. CODE § 5-71-301 to -303.
California. CAL. PENAL CODE § 11460.
Colorado. COLO. REV. STAT. § 18-9-120.
Connecticut. CONN. GEN. STAT. § 53-206b.
Michigan. MICH. COMP. LAWS § 750.528a.
Louisiana. LA. REV. STAT. ANN. § 117.1.
Missouri. MO. REV. STAT. § 574.070.
Montana. MONT. CODE ANN. § 45-8-109.
Nebraska. NEB. REV. STAT. § 28-1480 to -1482.
New Jersey. N.J. REV. STAT. § 2C:39-14.
New Mexico. N.M. STAT. ANN. § 30-20A-1 to -4.
Oklahoma. OKLA. STAT. ANN. tit. 21, § 1321.10.
Oregon. OR. REV. STAT. § 166.660.
Pennsylvania. 18 PA. CONS. STAT. § 5515.
South Carolina. S.C. CODE ANN. § 16-8-10 to -30.
Tennessee. TENN. CODE ANN. § 39-17-314.
Virginia. VA. CODE ANN. § 18.2-433.1 to -433.3.

Model Statutes to Prohibit
Militia Organizing and Anti-Paramilitary Training

Southern Poverty Law Center Model Anti-Militia Statute

This statute:

1. Outlaws private military organizations.

2. Enhances penalties for crimes committed under the auspices of private military organizations.

3. Exempts the National Guard, the Armed Forces of the United States, and other government-sanctioned entities.

4. Permits civil actions by prosecutors or private citizens.

TEXT:

A) It shall be unlawful for any person to assemble, associate, train, congregate or parade with other persons as a military organization in this State without the prior approval of the Governor.

B) Any individual violating this section shall be deemed guilty of a Class ___ misdemeanor.

C) Any individual violating this section who also is convicted of another state criminal offense while acting as a member of an unauthorized military organization shall have his or her sentence increased by one offense level for that offense in addition to any penalties accrued under subdivision B of this statute.

D) This statute shall not apply to persons engaged in the official activities of:

(1) the state National Guard;

(2) other state mandated military bodies;

(3) the duly authorized Armed Forces of the United States and Coast Guard;

(4) chapters of the Boy Scouts, the American Legion and Veterans of Foreign Wars;

(5) state sanctioned police departments and police academies;

(6) classes at accredited educational institutions where military science is a prescribed part of the course of instruction;

(7) any assembly for public historical reenactment purposes by a historic military reenactment group portraying events in military history presented for the purposes of public entertainment and education, provided that the reenactments be open to the public and the participants utilize historically appropriate uniforms, weapons, and accouterments;

(8) any group exempted or authorized by the Governor or the Commander of the State National Guard.

E) The Attorney General, any district attorney, or any city attorney may bring a civil action for injunctive and other appropriate relief in the name of the people of the State of _____ to cease the prohibited activities set forth in this statute.

F) Anyone injured by conduct prohibited in this statute may institute a civil action against the offending party(ies) for injunctive or other appropriate relief, including compensatory and punitive damages, as well as attorneys fees and costs.

G) As used in this statute, the term "military organization" means a group (a) operating under a formal or informal command structure; (b) consisting of armed persons or soldiers; (c) that drills with weapons; and (d) is reasonably capable of being readily assembled for unified independent service in armed conflict.

Southern Poverty Law Center
Model Anti-Paramilitary Training Statute

Terroristic Training

This statute:

1. Outlaws training to foment violent civil disorders.

2. Outlaws the transport or manufacture of weapons or explosives.

3. Outlaws interference with police and fire personnel during civil disorders.

TEXT:

A) Anyone who:

(1) instructs or demonstrates to another person the use, application, or making of any firearm or explosive or incendiary device, or technique capable of causing injury or death to persons, knowing or having reason to know or intending that the same will be unlawfully employed for use in, or in furtherance of, a civil disorder; or

(2) transports or manufactures for transportation any firearm, or explosive or incendiary device, knowing or having reason to know or intending that the same will be unlawfully used in furtherance of a civil disorder; or

(3) commits or attempts to commit any act to obstruct, impede, or interfere with any firefighter, law enforcement officer lawfully engaged in the lawful performance of his or her official duties incident to and during the commission of a civil disorder;

is guilty of Terroristic Training, a Class ___ Felony, punishable by up to ___ years of imprisonment or $___, or both.

B) Nothing contained in this section shall make unlawful any act of any law enforcement officer which is performed in the lawful performance of his or her official duties.

C) The Attorney General, or any district attorney, or city attorney may also bring a civil action for injunctive and other appropriate relief in the name of the people of the State of _____, to cease the prohibited activities set forth in this statute.

D) Anyone injured by conduct prohibited in this statute may institute a civil action against the offending party(ies) for injunctive or other appropriate relief, including compensatory and punitive damages, as well as attorneys fees and costs.

Anti-Defamation League
Model Anti-Paramilitary Training Statute

A.   (1) Whoever teaches or demonstrates to any other person the use, application, or making of any firearm, explosive, or incendiary device, or technique capable of causing injury or death to persons, knowing, or having reason to know or intending that same will be unlawfully employed for use in, or in furtherance of, a civil disorder; or

(2) Whoever assembles with one or more persons for the purpose of training with, practicing with, or being instructed in the use of any firearm, explosive or incendiary device, or technique capable of causing injury or death to persons, intending to employ unlawfully the same for use in, or in furtherance of, a civil disorder—

Shall be fined not more than $_____ or imprisoned not more than _____ years, or both.

B.   Nothing in this section shall make unlawful any act of any law enforcement officer which is performed in the lawful performance of his official duties.

C.   As used in this section:

(1) The term "civil disorder" means any public disturbance involving acts of violence by assemblages of three or more persons, which causes an immediate danger of or results in damage or injury to the property or person of any individual.

(2) The term "firearm" means any weapon which is designed to or may readily be converted to expel any projectile by the action of an explosive; or the frame or receiver of any such weapon.

(3) The term "explosive or incendiary device" means (a) dynamite and all other forms of high explosives, (b) any explosive bomb, grenade, missile, or similar device, and (c) any incendiary bomb or grenade, fire bomb, or similar device, including any device which (i) consists of or includes a breakable container including a flammable liquid

or compound, and a wick composed of any material which, when ignited, is capable of igniting such flammable liquid or compound, and (ii) can be carried or thrown by one individual acting alone.

(4) The term "law enforcement officer" means any officer or employee of the United States, any state, any political subdivision of a state, or the District of Columbia, and such term shall specifically include, but shall not be limited to, members of the National Guard, as defined in section 101(9) of title 10, United States Code, members of the organized militia of any state or territory of the United States, the Commonwealth of Puerto Rico, or the District of Columbia, not included within the definition of National Guard as defined by such section 101(9), and members of the Armed Forces of the United States.

Appendix C

Federal Anti-Paramilitary Training Statute

The Civil Disobedience Act of 1968
18 U.S.C. § 231

(a)(1) Whoever teaches or demonstrates to any other person the use, application, or making of any firearm or explosive or incendiary device, or technique capable of causing injury or death to persons, knowing or having reason to know or intending that the same will be unlawfully employed for use in furtherance of, a civil disorder which may in any way or degree obstruct, delay, or adversely affect commerce or the movement of any article or commodity in commerce or the conduct or performance of any federally protected function; or

(2) Whoever transports or manufactures for transportation in commerce any firearm, or explosive or incendiary device, knowing or having reason to know or intending that the same will be used unlawfully in furtherance of a civil disorder; or

(3) Whoever commits or attempts to commit any act to obstruct, impede, or interfere with any firearm or law enforcement officer lawfully engaged in the lawful performance of his official duties incident to and during the commission of a civil disorder which in any way or degree obstructs, delays, or adversely affects commerce or the conduct or performance of any federally protected function—

Shall be fined under this title or imprisoned not more than five years, or both.

(b) Nothing contained in this section shall make unlawful any act of any law enforcement officer which is performed in the lawful performance of his official duties.

Appendix D

Congress of the United States
House of Representatives

Stop Domestic Terrorism
Put an End to Private Armies

May 4, 1995

Dear Colleague,

Do your constitutents believe that private citizens should be allowed to organize themselves into private armies for the purpose of making war on the democratically elected government? Is this really how a free society makes its decisions?

If you are as concerned as I am about the formation of private armies, then I urge you to co-sponsor H.R. 1544, which would prohibit the formation of private paramilitary organizations with the intention of unlawfully opposing the authority of the United States or any State or for any other unlawful purpose.

The message we send must be clear—in a democracy, the way to change public policy is with ballots and not with bullets. The Constitution does not protect people who kill those entrusted to enforce the laws made by democratically elected representatives. This violent lawlessness is the real threat to our freedoms.

Some people have been warning for years that these private armies pose a real threat of violence. Unfortunately very few paid attention. Now that the tragic mass murder in Oklahoma City has brought this forcefully to our attention, it is time that Congress act to make our streets safe for democratic discourse and for law-abiding citizens. We must put these violence-prone private armies out of business once and for all.

Thank you for your consideration of this legislation.

Sincerely,

Jerrold L. Nadler

104TH CONGRESS
1ST SESSION

H.R. 1544

To prohibit the formation of private paramilitary organizations.

IN THE HOUSE OF REPRESENTATIVES

May 2, 1995

Mr. Nadler introduced the following bill;
which was referred to the Committee on the Judiciary

A BILL

To prohibit the formation of private paramilitary organizations.

Be it Enacted by the Senate and House of Representatives of the
United States of America in Congress assembled,

SECTION 1. SHORT TITLE

This Act may be cited as the "Domestic Insurgency Act of 1995."

SEC. 2. PARAMILITARY ORGANIZATIONS.

(a) IN GENERAL.—Chapter 115 of title 18, United States Code, is
amended by adding at the end the following:

"§ 2392. Paramilitary organizations

"(a) Whoever knowingly participates in a paramilitary organization
shall be fined under this title or imprisoned not more than 10 years, or
both.

"(b) As used in this section, the term 'paramilitary organization' means two or more individuals acting together, organized in a military or paramilitary structure, who knowingly—

"(1) possess firearms, explosives, incendiary devices, or other weapons or techniques capable of causing injury or death to individuals; or

"(2) provide or participate in training in the use of any such weapons or techniques;

with the intention that such weapons or techniques be used unlawfully to oppose the authority of the United States or of any State or for any other unlawful purpose.".

(b) CLERICAL AMENDMENT.—The table of sections at the begining of chapter 115 of title 18, United States Code, is amended by adding at the end the following new item:

"2392. Paramillitary organizations.".

104th CONGRESS
1ST SESSION

H.R. 1899

To amend title 18, United States Code, to prohibit certain conduct relating to civil disorders.

IN THE HOUSE OF REPRESENTATIVES
June 20, 1995

Mr. Nadler introduced the following bill; which was referred to the Committee on the Judiciary

A BILL

To amend title 18, United States Code, to prohibit certain conduct relating to civil disorders.

Be it enacted by the Senate and House of Representatives of the United States of America in Congress assembled,

SECTION 1. SHORT TITLE.

This Act may be cited as the "Domestic Counter Terrorism Act of 1995."

SEC. 2. CIVIL DISORDERS.

(a) IN GENERAL.—Section 231(a) of title 18, United States Code, is amended.—

(1) by striking the one-em dash at the end of paragraph (3) and inserting "; or";

(2) by inserting after paragraph (3) the following:

"(4) Whoever trains in the use, application, or making of any firearm or explosive or incendiary device, or technique capable of causing injury or death to persons, knowing or having reason to know or intending that the same will be unlawfully employed for use in or in furtherance of a civil disorder which—

"(A) may in any way or degree obstruct, delay, or adversely affect—

"(i) commerce or the movement of any article or commodity in commerce; or

"(ii) the conduct or performance of any federally protected function; or

"(B) is in violation of chapter 13 of this title.";

and

(3) in paragraph (1), by inserting "or is in violation of chapter 13 of this title" before the semi-colon.

(b) DEFINITION.— Paragraph (7) of section 232 of title 18, United States Code, is amended to read as follows:

"(7) The term 'law enforcement officer'—

"(A) means any officer or employee of the United States, any state, any political subdivision of a State, or the District of Columbia, while acting in the lawful scope of such officer or employee's duties;

"(B) includes members of the National Guard (as defined in section 101 of title 10), members of the organized militia of any State or territory of the United States, the Commonwealth of Puerto Rico, or the District of Columbia, not included within the National Guard (as so defined), and members of the Armed Forces of the United States while engaged in suppressing acts of violence or restoring law and order during a civil disorder.".

Appendix E

A History of State Militias in the United States
BY BRIAN LEVIN

Courtesy of the Klanwatch/Militia Task Force
of the Southern Poverty Law Center

Colonial Period: Militias take part in frontier battles against Native Americans and the French.

1774: The Minutemen, a volunteer regiment of citizens, is established by the Massachusetts Provisional Congress.

1775: On April 19, eight Minutemen are killed and ten are wounded by British "Redcoat" troops at Lexington, Massachusetts, in the first battle of the Revolutionary War. Colonial snipers retaliate, killing seventy-three Redcoat troops during the return of the British troops to Boston.

Pre-revolution Congress forms the Continental Army to establish a more effective and better regulated fighting force. The Continental Army replaces the volunteer militias, because the militias could not be relied upon to fight when needed or to follow a centralized chain of command.

In July, General George Washington becomes commander of the Continental Army. Militias aid the Continental Army during the Revolutionary War.

1789: The United States Constitution is ratified to "insure domestic tranquility, provide for the common Defence, [and to] promote the general welfare."

Article I, § 8 gives the Congress authority to "provide for the common Defence and general welfare of the United States." Congress is given authority over organizing, arming, and disciplining the militia when in federally mandated service, but the states retain power over the appointment of officers and the implementation of mandated training.

Article I, § 10 prohibits states from maintaining troops in peacetime without congressional approval.

Article II, § 2 establishes the president as commander in chief of the Armed Forces and of the state militias when they are called into federal service.

1791: The first ten amendments to the Constitution—"the Bill of Rights"—are ratified. The Second Amendment provides that "A well regulated Militia, being necessary to the security of a free State, the right of the people to keep and bear Arms, shall not be infringed."

1790s: Fearing that a large standing army would be "dangerous to the liberties of a free people," the Congress slashes the ranks of the army and proposes militia legislation.

1792: The Militia Act passes and establishes duties and membership requirements for state militias.

1795: New law sets out when the president may place the militia into federal service.

1800s: Influence of militia forces diminishes as they prove to be generally ineffective. Mandatory militia service, though technically required, is phased out.

1860s: Although voluntary militia units serve on both sides durinig the Civil War, most soldiers enlist in the army as individuals or are drafted.

1876: In *United States v. Cruikshank,* a case involving the prosecution of armed criminals under the new Ku Klux Klan Act, the United States Supreme Court states: "The right to bear arms is not granted by the Constitution."

1877: With the formation of the National Guard Association by state officials, state militias become known as the National Guard.

1886: In *Presser v. Illinois,* the United States Supreme Court upholds an Illinois state law prohibiting unauthorized military groups and parading with arms. The court rules that neither the First Amendment's guarantee of freedom of association nor the Second Amendment prevents states from banning unofficial militias.

1903: The Dick Act is enacted and establishes the modern National Guard. The National Guard is to be funded jointly by the individual states and the federal government. Subsequent legislation further addresses the funding of the National Guard and its duties.

1939: In *United States v. Miller,* the United States Supreme Court holds that the Second Amendment does not bar the federal government from prosecuting two defendants who shipped illegal sawed-off shotguns. The Court rules that the Second Amendment protections only were intended to preserve the effectiveness of official state militias.

1957: Proclaiming "mob rule cannot be allowed to overide the decisions of our courts," President Dwight Eisenhower federalizes the Arkansas National Guard as part of an overall military effort to curb violence that erupted after court-mandated desegregation.

1960s: President John Kennedy federalizes the National Guard troops in Alabama and Mississippi to maintain peace during the enforcement of desegregation orders.

1968: At the height of the Vietnam War, Congress enacts the Federal Civil Disobedience Act (18 U.S.C. § 231), prohibiting paramilitary-type instruction aimed at fomenting violent civil disorders and other related activities. Subsequent federal court decisions uphold the statute.

1970: New laws establish federal jurisdiction over bomb use and manufacture.

1982: In a lawsuit filed by the Southern Poverty Law Center, a federal district court rejects a challenge to Texas' anti-militia law and prohibits the Texas Emergency Reserve, a private paramilitary wing of the Ku Klux Klan, from operating. The paramilitary group had waged a terror campaign against immigrant fishermen. See *Vietnamese Fishermen's Association v. Knights of the Ku Klux Klan.*

1986: A federal district court in North Carolina, in a lawsuit filed by the Southern Poverty Law Center, issues a criminal contempt order against Klansmen Glenn Miller and Stephen Miller for operating an illegal paramitary group, the White Patriot Party. The contempt order halted the activities of the White Patriot Party and resulted in the group's dissolution. See *Person v. Miller.*

1990: In *Perpich v. Department of Defense,* the United States Supreme Court rules that the Constitution's Militia Clauses give the federal government ultimate authority to determine when state militias may be called for federal service.

1995: The Domestic Counter-Terrorism Act of 1995, H.R. 1899, is proposed in Congress. The proposal would strengthen the Federal Civil Disobedience Act by punishing all participants in paramilitary training, not just instructors.

1995: H.R. 1544 is proposed in Congress. The proposal would prohibit the formation of private paramilitary organizations.

Notes

1   The Militia Movement

1. ANTI-DEFAMATION LEAGUE, ARMED AND DANGEROUS: MILITIAS TAKE AIM AT THE FEDERAL GOVERNMENT 1 (1994).

2. THE AMERICAN JEWISH COMMITTEE, MILITIAS: A GROWING DANGER 1 (1995).

3. ANTI-DEFAMATION LEAGUE, PARANOIA AS PATRIOTISM: FAR-RIGHT INFLUENCES ON THE MILITIA MOVEMENT 4 (1995).

4. ANTI-DEFAMATION LEAGUE, BEYOND THE BOMBING: THE MILITIA MENACE GROWS 1 (1995).

5. *Over 200 Militias and Support Groups Operate Nationwide,* KLANWATCH INTELLIGENCE REPORT, June 1995, at 1.

6. Telephone conversation with Brian Levin, Associate Director of Legal Affairs, Klanwatch Project, Southern Poverty Law Center, February 1996.

7. ARMED AND DANGEROUS, *supra* note 1 at 2.

8. PARANOIA AS PATRIOTISM, *supra* note 3 at 11.

9. *Id.* at 9.

2   Militias and the Constitution   35

1. The Dick Act of Jan. 21, 1903, ch. 196, 32 Stat. 775.

2. The Militia Act of May 8, 1792, ch. 33, 1 Stat. 271.

3. 394 U.S. 705 (1969).

4. 395 U.S. 444 (1969).

5. *Id.*

6. 491 U.S. 397 (1989).

7. 274 U.S. 357 (1927).

8. THE AMERICAN JEWISH COMMITTEE, WHAT TO DO WHEN THE MILITIA COMES TO TOWN v, 22 (1995).

132

9. 343 U.S. 250 (1952).

10. 307 U.S. 174 (1939).

11. 445 U.S. 55 (1980).

12. The National Firearms Act of June 26, 1934, ch. 757, 48 Stat. 1236.

13. The Gun Control Act of June 19, 1968, 82 Stat. 1213 (codified as amended at 18 U.S.C. §§ 921-928 (1976)).

14. 307 U.S. 174 (1939).

15. 445 U.S. 55 (1980).

16. 978 F.2d 1016 (8th Cir. 1992).

17. 440 F.2d 144 (6th Cir. 1971).

18. 530 F.2d 103 (6th Cir.), *cert. denied,* 426 U.S. 948 (1976).

19. Keith A. Ehrman and Dennis A. Henigan, *The Second Amendment in the Twentieth Century: Have You Seen Your Militia Lately?,* 15 U. DAYTON L. REV. 5, 42-43 (1989).

20. The Federal Firearms Act of June 30, 1938, ch. 850, §§ 1-9, 52 Stat. 1250-52 (repealed 1968).

21. 131 F.2d 916 (1st Cir. 1942), *cert. denied sub nom., Velazquez v. United States,* 319 U.S. 770 (1943).

22. Ehrman and Henigan, *supra* note 19 at 44.

23. *Id.* at 19-20, 24.

24. Sanford Levinson, *The Embarrassing Second Amendment,* 99 YALE L.J. 637 (1989).

25. Dennis A. Henigan, *Guns and the Judiciary,* in GUNS AND THE CONSTITUTION: THE MYTH OF SECOND AMENDMENT PROTECTION FOR FIREARMS IN AMERICA 21 (Aletheia Press 1996).

26. WAYNE LAPIERRE, GUNS, CRIME AND FREEDOM 20 (1994).

27. Philip Weiss, *A Hoplophobe Among the Gunnies, N.Y. Times,* Sept. 11, 1994, § 6.

28. *Anti-Government Terrorism in the United States: Hearings on the Nature and Extent of the Threat and Possible Legislative Responses Before the Subcomm. on Crime of the House Judiciary Comm.,* 104th Cong., 1st Sess. (November 2, 1995) (Testimony of David Kopel, Associate Policy Analyst, Cato Institute).

29. *Id.*

30. 116 U.S. 252 (1886).

31. *Id.*

32. 543 F. Supp. 198 (S.D. Tex. 1982).

33. *Id.*

34. 51 N.Y.S.2d 202 (1944), *aff'd,* 73 N.E.2d 41 (1947).

35. 543 F. Supp. 198 (S.D. Tex. 1982).

36. KENNETH STERN, A FORCE UPON THE PLAIN: THE AMERICAN MILITIA MOVEMENT AND THE POLITICS OF HATE 233 (1996).

37. The Civil Disobedience Act of Apr. 11, 1968, 82 Stat. 90, 18 U.S.C. §§ 231-233.

38. *Over 200 Militias and Support Groups Operate Nationwide,* KLANWATCH INTELLIGENCE REPORT, June 1995, at 14.

Bibliography

Books

Aho, James A. *The Politics of Righteousness: Idaho Christian Patriotism.* Seattle, Wash.: The University of Washington Press, 1990.

Barkun, Michael. *Religion and the Racist Right: The Origins of the Christian Identity Movement.* Chapel Hill, N.C.: The University of North Carolina Press, 1994.

Blanchard, Dallas A., and Terry J. Prewitt. *Religious Violence and Abortion: The Gideon Project.* Gainesville, Fla.: The University of Florida Press, 1993.

Corcoran, James. *Bitter Harvest: Gordon Kahl and the Posse Comitatus: Murder in the Heartland.* New York: Penguin Books, 1990.

Dees, Morris. *A Season for Justice: The Life and Times of a Civil Rights Lawyer.* New York: Scibners, 1991.

Dees, Morris, and James Corcoran. *Gathering Storm: America's Militia Threat.* New York: HarperCollins, 1996.

Diamond, Sara. *Spiritual Warfare: The Politics of the Christian Right.* Boston: South End Press, 1989.

Dupuy, Ernest R. *The National Guard: A Short History.* New York: Hawthorne Books, Inc., 1971.

Flynn, Kevin, and Gary Gerhardt. *The Silent Brotherhood: Inside America's Racist Underground.* New York: The Free Press, 1989.

Gibson, James William. *Warrior Dreams: Paramilitary Culture in Post-Vietnam America.* New York: Hill and Wang, 1994.

Gunther, Gerald. *Individual Rights in Constitutional Law.* Westbury, N.Y.: Foundation Press, 1992.

Henigan, Dennis A., E. Bruce Nicholson, and David Hemenway. *Guns and the Constitution: The Myth of Second Amendment Protection for Firearms in America.* Amherst, Mass.: Aletheia Press, 1996.

LaPierre, Wayne. *Guns, Crime, and Freedom.* Washington, D.C.: Regnery, 1994.

McLean, Nancy. *Behind the Mask of Chivalry: The Making of the Second Ku Klux Klan.* New York: Oxford University Press, 1994.

Padilla, Lana, with Ron Delpit. *By Blood Betrayed: My Life with Terry Nichols and Timothy McVeigh.* New York: HarperCollins, 1995.

Reavis, Dick J. *The Ashes of Waco: An Investigation.* New York: Simon and Schuster, 1995.

Seymour, Cheri. *Committee of the States: Inside the Radical Right.* Mariposa, Calif.: Camden Place Communications, Inc., 1991.

Slotkin, Richard. *Gunfighter Nation: The Myth of the Frontier in Twentieth-Century America.* New York: HarperPerrenial, 1992.

Smith, Brent L. *Terrorism in America: Pipe Bombs and Pipe Dreams.* Albany, N.Y.: State University of New York Press, 1994.

Stern, Kenneth S. *A Force Upon the Plain: The American Militia Movement and the Politics of Hate.* New York: Simon and Schuster, 1996.

Sugarmann, Josh. *NRA: Money, Firepower, and Fear.* Washington, D.C.: National Press Books, 1992.

Sunstein, Cass. *Democracy and the Problem of Free Speech.* New York: The Free Press, 1993.

Tabor, James D., and Eugene V. Gallagher. *Why Waco: Cults and the Battle for Religious Freedom in America.* Berkeley, Calif.: University of California Press, 1995.

Walter, Jess. *Every Knee Shall Bow: The Truth and Tragedy of Ruby Ridge and the Randy Weaver Family.* New York: HarperCollins, 1995.

Law Journals

Ehrman, Keith and Dennis A, Henigan, *The Second Amendment in the Twentieth Century: Have You Seen Your Militia Lately?*, 15 U. DAYTON L. REV. 5 (1989).

Farfarman, *State Assault Rifle Bans and the Militia Clauses of the United States Constitution,* 67 IND. L.J. 187 (1991).

Henigan, Dennis A, *Arms, Anarchy, and the Second Amendment,* VAL. U.L. REV.

Levinson, Sanford, *The Embarrassing Second Amendment,* 99 YALE L.J. 637 (1989).

Reed, Scott W., *The County Supremacy Movement: Mendacious Myth Marketing*, 30 IDAHO L. REV. 525 (1994)

Van Alstyne, *The Second Amendment and the Personal Right to Arms*, 43 DUKE L.J. 1236 (1994)

Vandercoy, *The History of the Second Amendment*, 28 VAL. U.L. REV. 1007 (1994)

Williams, *Civic Republicanism and the Citizen Militia: The Terrifying Second Amendment*, 101 YALE L.J. 551 (1991).

Reports

Armed and Dangerous: Militias Take Aim at the Federal Government, New York: Anti-Defamation League, 1994.

Aryan World Congress Focuses on Militias and an Expected Revolution, Montgomery, Ala.: Klanwatch, August 1995.

Beyond the Bombing: The Militia Menace Grows, New York: Anti-Defamation League, 1995.

Firearms Regulations in Various Foreign Countries, Washington, D.C.: Law Library of Congress, 1990.

Militias: A Growing Danger, New York: The American Jewish Committee, April 1995.

Over 200 Militias and Support Groups Operate Nationwide, Montgomery, Ala.: Klanwatch, June 1995.

Paranoia as Patriotism: Far-Right Influences on the Militia Movement, New York: Anti-Defamation League, 1995.

Patriot Underground Strikes in '95, Montgomery, Ala.: Klanwatch, February 1996.

Prominent Militia Networks Launch Counter-Intelligence Campaign, Montgomery, Ala.: Klanwatch, October, 1995.

The ADL Anti-Paramilitary Training Statute: A Response to Domestic Terrorism, New York: Anti-Defamation League, 1995.

What to Do When the Militia Comes to Town, New York: The American Jewish Committee, November 1995.

False Patriots: The Growing Threat of Antigovernment Extremism, Montgomery, Ala.: Klanwatch, April, 1996.